HOW TO BE A DJ

Janet Hoggarth (aka Phat Biffa) is a pop-culture writer who started DJing when Mr Benn, her DJ husband, left her to cover for him mid-set while visiting the gents. She has been hooked ever since.

So far, her best DJ experience has been headlining at a media Christmas party and overhearing in the girls' toilet that everyone thought she was the best DJ they'd heard in ages. Her worst was her first-ever gig at the DogStar in Brixton when she didn't know how to work the mixer, almost smashed her records and threw a superstar DJ tantrum ...

HOW TO BE A DJ

J. HOGGARTH

**Illustrations by
Zac Sandler**

PENGUIN BOOKS

PENGUIN BOOKS

Published by the Penguin Group
Penguin Books Ltd, 80 Strand, London WC2R 0RL, England
Penguin Putnam Inc., 375 Hudson Street, New York, New York 10014, USA
Penguin Books Australia Ltd, 250 Camberwell Road, Camberwell, Victoria 3124, Australia
Penguin Books Canada Ltd, 10 Alcorn Avenue, Toronto, Ontario, Canada M4V 3B2
Penguin Books India (P) Ltd, 11 Community Centre, Panchsheel Park, New Delhi – 110 017, India
Penguin Books (NZ) Ltd, Cnr Rosedale and Airborne Roads, Albany, Auckland, New Zealand
Penguin Books (South Africa) (Pty) Ltd, 24 Sturdee Avenue, Rosebank 2196, South Africa

Penguin Books Ltd, Registered Offices: 80 Strand, London WC2R 0RL, England

www.penguin.com

First published 2002

1

Text copyright © Janet Hoggarth, 2002
Illustrations copyright © Zac Sandler, 2002
All rights reserved

The moral right of the author and illustrator has been asserted

Set in Helvetica

Made and printed in England by Clays Ltd, St Ives plc

Except in the United States of America, this book is sold subject to the condition
that it shall not, by way of trade or otherwise, be lent, re-sold, hired out, or otherwise
circulated without the publisher's prior consent in any form of binding or cover
other than that in which it is published and without a similar condition including
this condition being imposed on the subsequent purchaser

British Library Cataloguing in Publication Data
A CIP catalogue record for this book is available from the British Library

ISBN 0–141–31523–7

This book wouldn't have been possible without all the DJs, music-biz people and friends who have helped me along the way. Let it roll with the big-up thank yous: James Gillham for being a star, Judge Jules, Jon Lipton at Serious, Tom, Tom and Ollie from the Plagia-wrists, Prime Cuts for locking me out of his house at 2 a.m., Lisa Loud, DJ Paulette for the burnt croissants, Dee at Slice PR, Karl 'Tuff Enuff' Brown, Graham Gold at Kiss FM, Hugh and Wes at Plastic Fantastic Records – the BEST record shop ever, Jason Ellis at Positiva, Matt at Slice PR, Ali B at Capital Radio, Dean Evans, Bob 'mine's half a shandy' Bhamra, Miss Behavin', Femme Fatal, Brandon Block, St.John de Zilva at DJ Workshop, Jill Thompson at Trust the DJ, Fiona Wraith – the Kindergarten Klub is nothing without you, DJ Leon from Flex FM, Alex Griffiths from Burnitblue, and all the crew at Penguin (Amanda, Sholto, Pippa, Clare, Tony, Leah and Katie).

Of course, I would be beaten up if I didn't dedicate this book to my husband, the best DJ ever, Mr Benn. It is all his fault that I am now a sleeve-pulling, let-me-go-on-the-decks bore. Pete, this is for you. xx

Important note on web sites

We've done our very best to make sure that the online information listed in this book is as appropriate, accurate and up to date as possible at the time of going to press. However, information on the Internet is liable to change. Web-site addresses and web-site content are constantly being updated and sites occasionally close down. In addition, there is the possibility that some web sites may contain material or links to material that may be unsuitable for children. Parents are strongly advised to ensure that children's access to the Internet is supervised by a responsible adult.

The publishers cannot accept responsibility for any third-party web sites or any material contained in or linked to the same or for any consequences arising from use of the Internet. Nor can we guarantee that any web site or URL shown in this book will be exactly as shown. If you wish to comment on a web site that is listed in this book, e-mail us at popular.culture@penguin.co.uk

contents

so, you wanna be a dj...? 1

chapter one
thank you for the music 5

chapter two
the technical bit 29

chapter three
it's all in the mix 55

chapter four
your scratching arsenal 81

chapter five
let's get this party started 105

chapter six
it's show time 123

last word 137

glossary 139

index 148

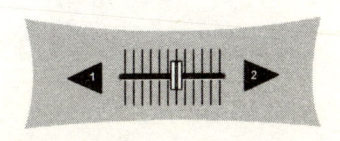

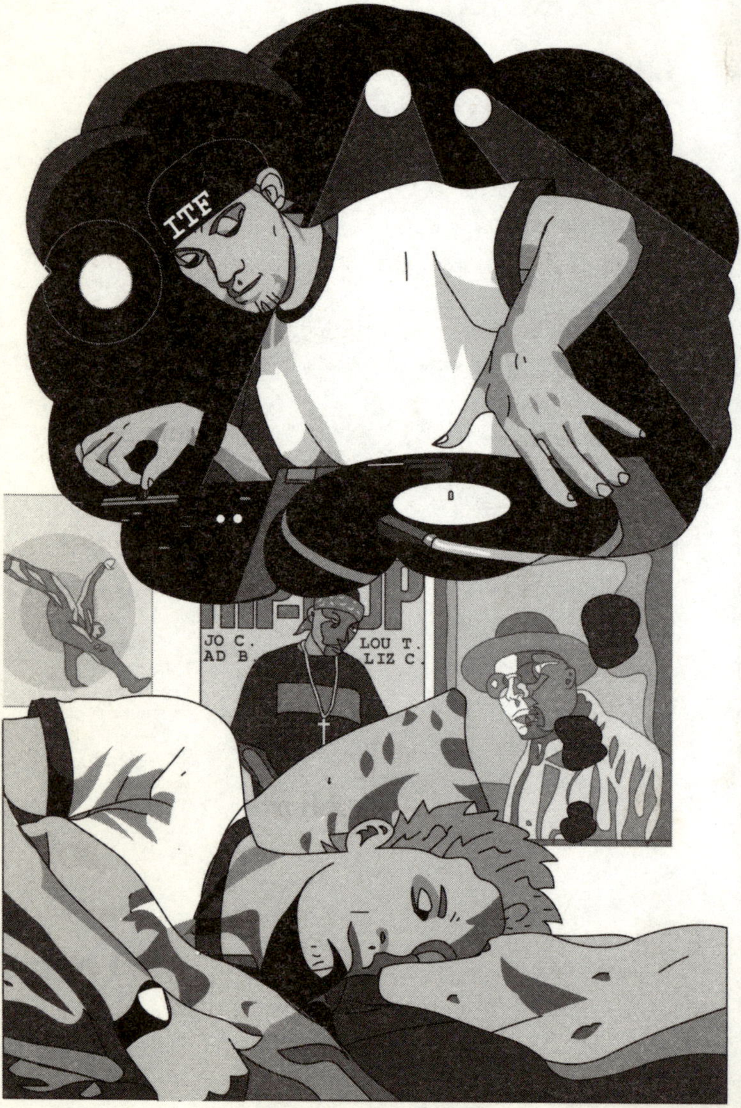
ITE
JO C.
AD B.
LOU T.
LIZ C.

so, you wanna be a dj...?

"That's the number one reason for getting into DJing – the fun!"
– ali b, capital radio

Picture the scene: you can feel the crowd hanging on to your every move, watching you, wanting you to bring in a tune that they know will lift them to another level, make them have a better time. You want to change the way a room feels, share your love of a great record, one that makes the hairs stand up on the back of your neck. You want everyone to love it as much as you do, and wave their hands in the air and shout with excitement. You are the DJ in control, you can do ... (Sound of needle scratching across record.)

WAKE UP! It was a dream – the same one you had last night and the night before and ever since you saw that guy looking cool on the TV, behind some decks, whipping up the crowd into a frenzy. You saw it happen and you thought, I want to do that. But WHEN are you going to do something about it, huh? You've got all those records in your bedroom and nothing to play them on, apart from some rubbish old wind-up thing left over from the Ark. It's time to take a good look through this book and check out everything that you could possibly need to know about DJing: the skillz, the music, the equipment, the time (you need LOTS of this because it'll take ages to perfect those mixing and scratching moves), money (DJing *doesn't* have to cost the earth; there are always cheaper alternatives available), and persistence – you'll need about a tonne of this, for sure. Just when you think you want to give it up, sell the decks and mixer to anyone who'll have them, you need a little voice at the back of your head to say: 'Oi, John, no! Stop that, it's silly. Get back on them decks and keep practising. Rome weren't built in a day, my son.' Persistence is what you need most of all. It doesn't matter if you have all the right records, equipment and time in the world, if you have no staying power, this isn't for you.

Remember that bit of advice if you can. The book is full of it – advice, that is – from some of the world's top DJs. They didn't all start out being superstars, you know. Most of them started off playing in youth clubs or to one man and his dog in a pub on a Wednesday night for a free pint and a packet of ready salted crisps. (Well, Brandon Block from Kiss FM did.) Some DJs are so young, they're *still* playing in youth clubs, DJ Kingy, for example (more about you young 'uns later). But all the big DJs had lots of persistence and succeeded where others failed, and sold their decks to buy a Volvo. Most of them were working as well as DJing, and **Karl 'Tuff Enuff' Brown** reckons everyone should ***'get a regular job to keep you going while you try and make it'***. Lisa Loud sold life assurance. Sasha worked in a fish factory. Timmi Magic made sparks fly as an electrician. Yousef worked for a catalogue company. Lottie was a sales assistant in agnès b. And they all made it! So, while you chop another onion or go on to sell another lot of shares on the stock market, keep working towards that goal ...

But before we go down the road to your first gig, you've got to get the equipment, haven't you? So I hope you have a paper round that covers the whole of Liverpool to pay for it, or at least parents willing to lend you the money, or maybe you have been really good this year and Santa has chucked two Technics down the chimney?

DJ Paulette from Ministry of Sound digital radio has a few wise words to say: ***'If you have a friend who has decks, practise on theirs. Maybe you could do it as a pair – share the cost. There's always ways of making it cheaper.'*** There *are* ways to make it cheaper and we'll check them out too in other chapters. DJ schools, for instance, are a good way to get on a pair of decks without paying a single penny. Read on for more info later in the book ...

Once you've got your ones and twos and a mixer sorted, that's when you can let loose and check out your ability to mix up a storm. But if all you can mix at this stage is a cake, and even then it comes out flat from the oven, fear not, help is at hand with our easy-to-follow basic skills and exclusive inside knowledge. Want Paul Oakenfold's secret top mixing tip? You betcha – it's here in black and white.

Maybe scratching's your bag and you fancy yourself as a bit of a turntablist? Then cut to the scratch chapter and feast your eyes on moves brought to you by the Plagia-wrists, while World DMC Champion Prime Cuts tears it up with some cool disses and sound words on the turntablist scene.

But hang on, there's still so much you need to know – what are all the genres of music? How do I get records if I live on the moon? Should I have an image? How do I get on record mailing lists? What else do I need to know apart from mixing or scratching to be a DJ? Persistence! (You will be amazed how often this word comes up in the book!) You *will* find out, just read the book, cover to cover, and we guarantee the fog will lift, or at least fade to a very thin mist.

So, now that you know this isn't going to be an easy ride (but a humungously worthwhile one!), are you still onboard the DJ Express? Only because our first stop is the music chapter, so get ready to be blinded by genres and get to know your house from your UK garage and your drum'n'bass from your hip-hop. Check, check, check, check it out ...

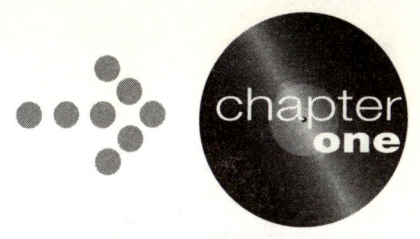

thank you for the music

❝I was always totally obsessed by music. I remember Mum putting a lock on the music-room door. Her records were special ... ❞ – dj paulette

history lesson one – know what you're playing

*'I really do think with the wealth of music out there right now and the many categories, and club land being segregated into different areas (with one music policy

***somewhere and another one somewhere else), that this has to be the other ingredient that you have to be totally sure about: where you fit'* – Lisa Loud**

There has always been a big debate about labelling genres of music and calling a certain sound one thing and another sound something else. In the UK this is very much the case (less so in America), with different nights, all over the country, promoting techno, house, deep house, UK garage, US garage, drum'n'bass, hip-hop, progressive house, old skool, breakbeat, big beat, trance, trip-hop, hard house, jungle, R & B – I could go on and on and on. But by the time this book is out, there will be a new genre on the block, ready to take the industry by storm and another favourite will be banished to the dance-music grave-yard, thrown there by music journalists telling us that trance/house/garage etc. is dead, long live deep garage speed trance with a bit of dog house and huge strop thrown in for good measure. All new genres are usually spin-offs of more mainstream dance music – so everything is linked somewhere down the line!

Before you go shopping for records, take some time to go on a lightning tour of the history of dance music, in the days before too many labels were stuck on with gloopy glue …

rappers' delight – hip-hop in a nutshell

Hip-hop culture has been around since the early 1970s and it encompasses graffiti art, MCing (rapping), dancing (breakdancing, up-rocking, body popping and locking) as well as DJing (cutting and scratching). The music part came about from kids in the New York Bronx setting up block parties, consisting of a DJ with two turntables, a microphone and a huge sound system playing records to a crowd. Instead of playing the whole record, DJs like Kool DJ Herc and Afrika Bambaataa (the founding father of hip-hop) would buy two copies of the same record and repeat the drum sections on either turntable in order to elongate the disco and funk breaks (the drums) to keep the party dancing. At the same time, an MC would 'toast' or rap over the mashed-up beats, creating a whole new sound.

It seemed natural that records recreating this new sound would follow, and the first official hip-hop or rap record was The Fatback Band's *King Tim III*

(Personality Jock). But most people actually think it was *Rappers' Delight* by the Sugarhill Gang, only because this tune was a massive hit and launched hip-hop into the mainstream. Other famous groundbreaking records were *Planet Rock* by Afrika Bambaataa, *Adventures on the Wheels of Steel* and *The Message* by Grandmaster Flash and the Furious Five. These were also big chart successes and paved the way for modern-day hip-hop, a billion-dollar industry that has created such massive stars as Eminem, Dr Dre, P Diddy, Dilated Peoples, Missy Elliot, Busta Rhymes and Jay-Z.

the house that jack built – house music

This takes its name from the Chicago Warehouse, opened in 1977, where a mishmash of disco and soul, underpinned by an additional drum machine (to give a kick like a mule and fortify the four-beat bass line) was played to an appreciative crowd. This constant beat made it easier to mix seamlessly from one track to another and thus drove the punters wild! DJ Frankie Knuckles, along with another DJ, Ron Hardy, pushed the sound of house music, as it was now being called, towards dizzy heights.

In 1984 the first house record was released – *On and On* by Jesse Saunders, a Chicago DJ, influenced by Frankie Knuckles and his use of the drum machine.

It was a success and opened the floodgates to everyone with a drum machine and a four-track tape recorder at home! From here on the sound grew, and it infiltrated the UK charts in 1986 with *Love Can't Turn Around* by Farley Jackmaster Funk and later, *Jack Your Body*.

These records inspired a young English guy, DJ Pierre, whose track *Acid Trax* went on to become an acid-house anthem and kick-started the craze of the same name. The rest, as they say, is history: Ibiza, M25 raves, the rise of the Superstar DJ and the gradual mutation of house music into different genres, so that now there are too many to shake a stick at: hard house, progressive house, handbag house, deep house, tech house and the rest.

detroit techno and european trance

Again, this style of music was spawned in the US, this time in Detroit. Derrick May, Kevin Saunderson and Juan Atkins were inspired by the funky computer sound of Kraftwerk (1980s' German group) and the house music coming out of Chicago, so they set themselves up as DJs, playing the party scene. But it was when they made music together that the word 'techno' started to get bandied about by music journalists because they fused both styles of music.

Kevin Saunderson went on to have hit singles with

Big Fun and *Good Life* as Inner City in 1988 – they were very poppy techno. But in the 1990s, the genre returned to the European roots of Kraftwerk, with records like *Energy Flash* from DJ Joey Beltram. DJs today that are known for playing techno, among other styles, are Carl Cox and Paul Oakenfold.

From techno, came trance, with its wobbly and bleepy noises, pounding four-to-the-floor bass line, uplifting and climactic snare-drum roll and some obligatory cheesy sci-fi flick sample thrown in. Ooh – and look out for Goa trance – popular in, errr, Goa, of all places …

love is the message – glorious us garage

Two DJs are responsible for the sound of US garage: Larry Levan from the Paradise Garage in New York and Tony Humphries from the Zanzibar Club in New Jersey.

Larry's sound was more of a melting pot of different styles, including rock music, old soul records, 80s' hits and funked-up disco, but he also remixed records and gave them that Paradise Garage sound, like *I Got My Mind Made Up* by Instant Funk.

Meanwhile, Tony Humphries (who had a real influence on Radio One's Danny Rampling) was spinning records with a strong gospel vocal emphasis – all very hands in the air. In-between what Larry and

Tony were playing, a sound was born – garage. It had the same feel as the uplifting house tracks that were emerging, but with more soulful leanings, jazzy instrumentals, complex up-tempo beats and with the main emphasis being on the diva-like voice of the singer. Such records were *You're Gonna Miss Me* by Adeva and *Make My Body Rock* by Jomanda. This sound was only a small selection of the records Larry played at the Garage, but the genre was named after the club anyway – a bit galling since Tony Humphries championed the music even more than Larry. But Zanzibar music doesn't have the same ring, does it? If you want to check out the sound of the Paradise Garage and the Chicago Warehouse, log on to www.deephouse.com.

drum'n'bass and jungle

Jungle was a UK phenomenon and took its influence from the early rave scene, with its banging hard acid house, hard techno (electronic drum-break music) and hip-hop. To put it very simply, it sounds like a speeded-up version of all those sounds, with an added ragga vocal (rather like Shaggy's voice, but without the reggae beat) and a bass line that would cave your chest in.

As its popularity grew through the 1990s, a load of sub-genres mushroomed (hard step, tech step, jump up, hardcore, happy hardcore and ambient, to name a few) and a new umbrella term was coined to keep them all dry: drum'n'bass. This new genre was easy to distinguish: it didn't have a four-to-the-floor bass line in a sequence like other genres; it used two or more different rhythms simultaneously. It was usually instrumental, with emphasis on the breakbeats, though a vocal will sometimes be sampled and the bass lines in most cases will still make you feel like you are vibrating from the inside out.

Goldie is the most famous DJ to bring drum'n'bass to the masses, with his *Timeless* album and in particular, the track *Inner City Life* (which was over twenty minutes' long!). Other notables are Fabio and Grooverider, and LTJ Bukem, who has a more ambient mellow sound – stuff that you might chill to.

Another genre sheltering under this umbrella is big beat. In a nutshell, this uses the drum breakbeats with a funky techno overlay on top, with breaks (instrumentals) taken from old soul or ska records – actually, anything that can be chopped up and used, really. Fat Boy Slim is the king of this genre, having massive chart success yet still managing to keep his credibility hat on.

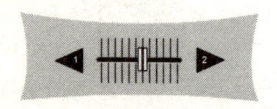

bo selector – uk garage

In the 1990s, DJs Matt 'Jam' Lamont, Karl 'Tuff Enuff'

Brown and the Dreem Teem from Radio One (Timmi Magic, Mikee B and DJ Spoony) were playing to audiences in the UK who wanted a new sound instead of the usual house or drum'n'bass. What they got was a fusion of US garage, R & B, reggae dub (instrumental) with the beats per minute speeded up. Tunes that typify the beginnings of the scene are DJ Armand Van Helden's mix of the Sneaker Pimp's tune *Spin, Spin Sugar* and Rosie Gains's *Closer Than Close*. This spin-off was called speed garage, but two step, the sound we know now as UK garage, wasn't far behind.

The music took a step (literally) further towards sugary R & B, and the record that pushed it there was Tina Moore's *Never Gonna Let You Go*. The vocals could have been taken from an R & B record and the bass line was missing two beats – hence the name. Suddenly, after beginning as a very London-based scene, UK garage exploded, with artists like Craig David, True Steppers and Dane Bowers, Mis-Teeq, Daniel Bedingfield, So Solid Crew and anyone else who wanted to be known as a 'UK garage' artiste (a certain someone married to an English footballer ...). Re-rewind ...

what's your bag?
'What music from the heart do you love? And do you want to play for your friends or

to the crowds? What do you want to be known for? Once you've got a really strong idea about records that make you feel a certain way then you should know why you are playing them. You've got to know why you're playing a record, otherwise what's the point?' **Ali B** hits the nail on the head. Think about it – why play progressive house, just because it is what is 'in' at the moment if you hate it? **Judge Jules** reckons a mistake lots of young DJs make while starting out is, ***'playing what they feel they're expected to play rather than what actually turns them on.'*** The key to being a good DJ is playing what you love – isn't that why you wanted to buy your decks in the first place? Loving what you are playing will translate to the crowd – showing your enthusiasm will infect them too, making the night a good one.

However, as Lisa Loud indicates at the beginning of the chapter, if you really want to make a serious impact with your DJing, you should probably have some sort of niche.

For example, Danny Rampling is known for playing funky US house and garage, the Dreem Teem play UK garage, Fergie plays hard house, as does Lisa Lashes and Lisa Pin Up, Lottie spins funky house, Bobby and Steve and Karl 'Tuff Enuff' Brown all mix up a selection of house, US and UK garage. The list is endless – as you can see, most big-name DJs are synonymous with a style of music.

But just because you start off with one style of music doesn't mean you have to stick with it forever – people and tastes can change. Judge Jules started off playing and promoting rare groove (soul classics and funk) and fellow Radio One DJ Dave Pearce started off as a hip-hop DJ before he became the cheesiest DJ on the block. The Dreem Teem were big players in the rave scene in the 80s' mixing up house, and Brandon Block used to play much harder stuff, but is now making his way back to his disco and soul roots with funky house.

Not all DJs have a clear-cut sound that people can label. Mr Scruff, a Stockport DJ, plays what is called in the business an 'eclectic' selection of tunes, picking what he likes from different places, but always with a similar vibe – music that makes you feel good. His Keep it Unreal nights are packed because there are thousands of clubbers out there who are very open-minded, and the thought of listening to a whole night of progressive house would bore them stupid.

However, Mr Scruff is a bit of an exception to the rule and you will find it hard to get real gigs playing stuff like that at first, even if it is what you truly love! Sometimes you do have to make a compromise and concentrate on one or two styles, rather than three or four, so you can get a gig, but always make sure the music is a style you love. **Femme Fatale**, resident at Garage Nation, tried everything before she found her niche: *'I think I went through every type of music: indie, house (all sorts), drum'n'bass etc ...'* You could do the same, if you're serious about making it professionally – try on everything for size and see what fits. As you get more established, you can bring different influences into your sets if that's what you want to do, and sometimes it is a good way to get noticed and make the crowd remember you – but we will cover playing for the crowd in chapter six. For now, let's concentrate on getting a feel for the tunes and buying them.

ooooh – me spine's all tingly

Many people try to get into DJing because they think it will get them attention from girls or boys – and there is nothing wrong with that! Or they think they will get rich and famous and be a celebrity. That could very well happen too. But it really helps if you have that underlying foundation of a love of music, bordering on the obsessional, to make it as a DJ. All major DJs sleep, eat, walk and talk music. Judge Jules listens to tunes about ten to twenty hours a week in case a few diamonds are lurking in the great piles he gets sent. ***'The excitement of being in a shop and hearing a record and thinking, Wait till they hear this one! There's nothing better – that is the number one reason for getting into DJing'*** – **DJ Ali B**. It's all about being chosen by the music. A tune seeks you out, crying, 'Buy me, take me, listen to my drum roll and twisted bass line, you know you wanna …' and you are compelled to track it down and helplessly hand over the cash. That passion is something you can't fake and if you have that feeling, then we are already halfway there!

calling all music geeks!

Truth time! Are you prepared to stand up and admit you have trainspottery tendencies when it comes to music? Do this quick Yes/No quiz to get a diagnosis:

a) Do the hairs on the back of your neck stand up when you hear certain tunes?

b) Do you want to tell everyone about your latest purchase so you can talk about it even more?

c) Are charity shops Aladdin's caves to you? An undiscovered cornucopia of unplayed white labels could be lurking in there, waiting for you to rescue them ...

d) Is your bedroom knee-deep in vinyl and CDs – so much so, you haven't seen the bed for two years?

e) Do you spend every penny you have on tunes, and thus have no clothes, no teeth, no friends or a girlfriend/boyfriend?

the verdict: If you answered yes to more than one of these questions, then you are a Music Obsessive. Nurse, quick, we have some more! Take them away ...

records to mix with

St.John de Zilva, a tutor at DJ Workshop and Fabric DJ in London says, *'It's always best to engage people on their terms – to learn on whatever they want to listen to.'* This theme keeps cropping up – no matter what, play music you love. **DJ Leon** from Flex FM says the same: *'I learned with house music; it is easier. But it's more important to learn with what you enjoy. There's no point playing music you don't like just because you think you might get better at it.'* One word of advice though, if you do have an eclectic taste and want tunes to learn to mix with, it is better to collect records with a similar bass line. There is nothing wrong with learning to mix all the different styles, but if you're into drum'n'bass more than garage, or two step more than trance, I would lean towards one genre for learning. You can always fiddle around later when you have grasped the basics. That's enough on mixing or I won't have anything left to say in chapter three. Like that will happen …

cd vs vinyl – the showdown

So we've established that you are a music geek, and that you should play music you love. But what if you can't decide what medium to play – in other words, vinyl or CD? Most DJs use both, but some, like **Brandon Block**, won't use CDs: *'I've not got the attitude for it. I'm not saying I'm stupid or thick – I don't have the vibe for it.'*. But CDs are fast becoming as much a part of DJing as vinyl. With the new mixers out now, **DJ Leon** reckons, *'The knives*

are out!' Roger Sanchez is the face of Pioneer and promotes the CDJ 1000, a revolutionary CD player that manipulates CDs like vinyl (see chapter two). He incorporates CDs into his sets all the time.

is vinyl better than cd? let's find out ...

In the red corner we have vinyl, whose vital statistics are as follows:

● Every single club in the world will have at least two turntables, so you can guarantee if you learn on vinyl, you will be able to play anywhere. Not every club has CD decks.

● Some people find that learning to mix on vinyl can be harder than on CD because record decks are not as exact and digital as CD decks. You don't have to worry about warped records or jumping needles while scratching (there are CD decks that you can scratch with).

Ali B isn't a fan of CDs, but does use them: *'Although it's good to go down that route of CDs, you are kinda getting closer to the territory of being a bit too digital for my liking. You can get MP3 mixers and any muppet can use them; it takes the fun out of it. My dad could use it and he can't even programme the video!'*

BUT, the plus point of this is, if you learn to mix on vinyl, the transition to learning on CD will be a lot easier than the other way round. **St.John de Zilva** agrees: *'If kids want to break into club mixing, then they should learn on vinyl first. Clubs have CD mixers, but there's something about vinyl. I don't know whether it's a cultural thing. It's about touching the vinyl – you get a different kind of mix too.'*

Other plus points:

● If a record jumps, it is easy to fix instantly. If a CD jumps and there is no anti-shock on the CD player, it is not easy to fiddle with.

🔘 Most of the new tracks (not promos) coming out are released straight on to vinyl, rather than CD.

🔘 Vinyl looks sexier! But that's just my opinion. Am I weird …?

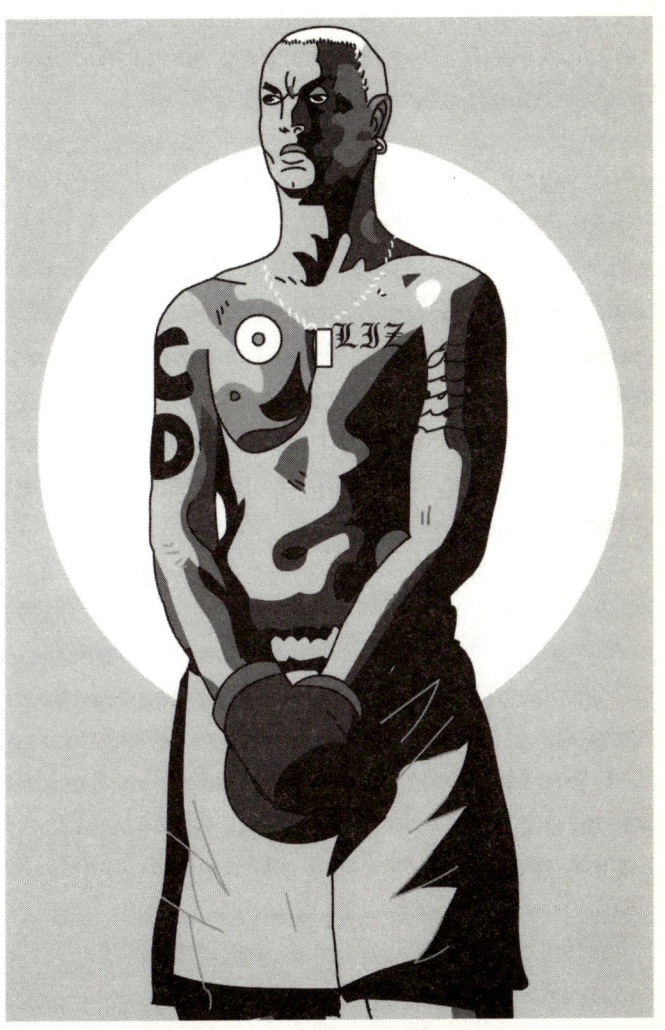

And in the blue corner we have CD, contending for the title of The DJ's Favourite. Its vitals are:

- CDs are a lot smaller, thus easier to transport than vinyl. Ever tried lugging a box of a hundred records anywhere?
- Vinyl promos are still going strong, but CDs are too. As **Graham Gold** puts it: ***'I don't CD mix but I should! It saves getting acetates cut and is much cheaper.'*** If a DJ makes their own music at home or in the studio, they'll want to test their tune on a dance floor. If they have a CD burner they can just burn it on to a CD (called a CD recording or CDR) there and then. If you don't use CDs, you have to get what is known as an acetate cut. It is a direct cutting from the tune you made on to a disc coated with acetate. It will only last about thirty plays at the most before it is knackered and will cost £30! CDs cost around £1 and last longer than normal vinyl too.

So, if CDs are cheaper to burn and so much less time-consuming to make, that means that promos come out on CD quicker than the acetate can be cut. ***'I get sent CDRs from producers I respect and I always use them whenever I can because when you do, you are being up-front, and you're being educational'*** – **Lisa Loud**

- Also, CDs hold time perfectly. There is no 'fluttering', where the decks speed up or slow down slightly, which can throw a mix.

The outcome: there is no clear winner. CD and vinyl both have their pros and cons. There is always going to be someone who prefers one over the other, but one thing is for sure: CDs are here to stay. But don't worry, vinyl – we still love you. Always.

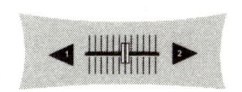

let's hit the shops

To know the right tunes and seek them out isn't as easy as you think. It's a good idea to tape your favourite radio dance shows so you can listen to them when you aren't going to be distracted. You can hear the tunes and the names of the artists properly and won't have to look for half-scribbled song titles on old bus tickets and English essays. Read all the magazines you can for reviews or check the web for music sites like www.burnitblue.com, but in the end, it will be your ears that'll tell you if a tune is great or not. So get thee to a record shop.

Don't be daunted by all the genres and sub-genres. If you have an idea of what you want to listen to, just go and ask someone. **Wes** at award-winning shop Plastic Fantastic Records in London says it doesn't matter if you are a bit unsure, let them help you. *'I'll start off asking them what sort of music they play or what artist or DJ they heard on the radio and liked the sound of. Then I'll dig out a big pile of records and get them to pick what they want from it.'*

Always listen before you buy – most decent record

shops have decks so you can try out tunes. Take your time, don't be intimidated by people and don't buy stuff you are unsure about while starting out, as you don't want to waste your hard-earned cash on something you may well decide is rubbish when you get home. Later on, when you are more experienced, you can take a gamble and buy something that might be a grower.

You can buy albums to save money and get more tunes, but be careful, as some are pressed at a quieter volume than twelve-inch recordings. That means when you are mixing an album track into a twelve-inch the sound level will change, unless you can crank up the volume. Look out for albums that say 'DJ friendly' and you will be OK. With CD albums, make sure you don't buy the mixed ones because they will be no use to you.

Don't forget the major chain stores too, where you can pick up some older tunes that you've heard about that the smaller, more on-the-ball shops won't stock, so go see.

on-line shopping

Of course, not everyone lives near a decent record store, so the easiest way to get records if you live in the Outer Hebrides is to do so on the Net. Hard to Find Records (www.htfr.com) have a great web site and it carries all genres, including hip-hop. Dance Music

Finder (www.dmf.co.uk) is another one that has a broad range of tunes. My favourite is Plastic Fantastic (www.plasticfantastic.co.uk). Just do a search on the Net and type in 'dance music stores' and see what comes up – you will discover that all genres of music are catered for. The good thing about buying on the web is that you can hear the tunes first, so you know what you are getting!

blagging promos!

Free promotional mailing lists are run by special promotion companies. Record labels send them all their new releases and the promotion companies send out the records/CDRs to DJs on their list. The idea is that the DJs play them out in clubland, so the tune builds up a following and possibly becomes a hit. Everyone wants to be on one because it means getting free records that haven't been released (or may never be). BUT, they are notoriously difficult to get on if you've had no DJing experience. There are lists that you can pay to join, but they can be expensive. However, at www.hooj.com you can buy vouchers in books of five and ten and it costs under a fiver for a CD.

But what about the FREE mailing lists? **Jason Ellis**, Head of A & R at Positiva Records, a large dance-music label, explains: ***'A good place to*** *start is probably the bigger promotion companies. Basically all they want to see is the number of people you are playing to in a week. If you are playing to four people in your bedroom, they won't put you on the list. But you don't have to have a huge following.'* The best thing to do is ring up your fave record companies and ask who you need to speak to in order to get on the mailing lists. They will probably refer you to the promotions company that does it for them.

If you live in a big town where there are lots of clubs, you probably don't stand much chance of getting on one. But if you live somewhere that record labels can't reach and want to (the moon, maybe?) then you might be able to talk them into it. You have to have a lot of front to do this, but **Ali B** has a tip that might help you on the way: *'They want evidence of you playing out – flyers and things. These days, with a bit of Photoshop, there's nothing to stop you making your own.'* For more advice on home-made flyers, see page 108/9.

As promoter **Fiona Wraith**, founding member of the Kindergarten Klub, points out, nothing is for nothing: *'You will only be allowed to continue on the lists if you review the records and send back your comments on the reaction slips. It is a big commitment and the music might not be what you're into, but it pays*

out as you move up the lists, from the bottom on to the bigger labels.' Good luck with those flyers …

take good care of me

Now you've got some decent tunes, look after them! CDs can fit anywhere, but vinyl is a bit more temperamental. Always store records upright, never in piles on top of each other, and keep them away from direct heat or sunlight. Radiators can warp records from one side if they are stored next to one. Lastly, buy a record bag to carry them in – nothing fancy, just something strong enough to keep them from getting broken.

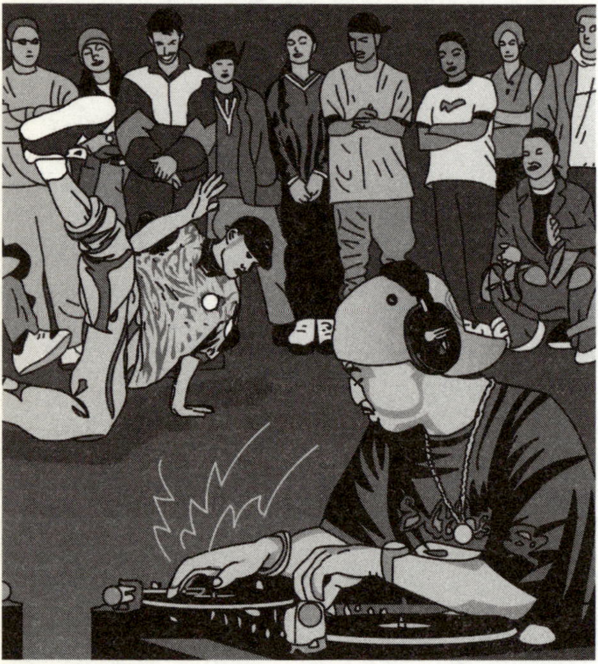

chapter two

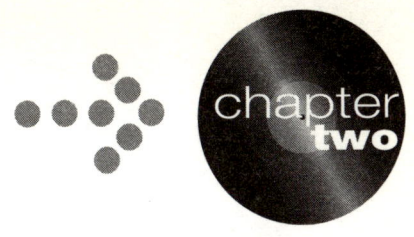

the technical bit

I had an old disco console first, which was very naff, but made me the envy of my mates – for about five minutes!
– judge jules

You may well know your way around a deck, know how to plug it all in and what all the buttons and faders and flashing lights are for, but some people don't, so this bit is for them. You might want to read it too, just in case you pick up something you didn't know that might come in handy for other chapters. But, before we begin the lesson, don't forget to show a bit of consideration to your neighbours and your family. They may not share your love of technotrancetriphophouse, so keep those volume levels down as much as possible.

first there were decks

There are two types of decks you can buy: direct-drive or belt-driven. EVERYBODY and I mean everybody in this book recommends you buy direct-drive. But if you do already own a set of belt-driven decks – don't chuck them out just yet as we give you mixing tips on how to get the most out of these decks in chapter three.

Belt-driven decks are what they sound like – the platter is spun round underneath by a motor and a thick rubber band, while direct-drive turntables are spun round by a direct motor. You will hear the term 'torque' bandied about when people talk about decks and basically this is the measurement of how powerfully a turntable is driven by the motor underneath the platter. For example, when you put your hand on a spinning record on a belt-driven deck, the record will slow down slightly because the motor and belt spinning the platter aren't as powerful (it has a low torque) as the motor on a direct-drive – meaning the power generated by the motor is going via a rubber band rather than straight to the platter, thus diluting the force. So on a direct-drive the high level of torque will keep the platter spinning at the same speed and there will be no variation at all, making it easier for cueing up records and mixing. Also, if you want to scratch, direct-drives are a must, though ITF Word Champ **Prime Cuts** remembers: *'As a kid I was scratching on an Amstrad stack system. I hated it because it had a volume control you pressed and there was no way of cutting out the sound. There was a linear tone arm that travelled across the record – it was no good for scratching.'*

The most popular makes you can get are Technics SL1200, 1210 or SL1210 Mk2 and Vestax PDX 2000. Technics are the industry standard – most clubs have them, though Vestax are installed in some clubs now (and lots of DJs reckon they are better). But in the Ministry of Sound's case, Stanton STR8-100 decks rule the DJ booth there. However, no one recommends you start out with these makes, apart from those who have forgotten what it is like to be poor and only have a Saturday job to get by on, as prices can vary between £700 and £800 a pair . . . Gulp!

Don't worry if you can't afford expensive decks, as every single DJ in the book started on low-grade kit, and you *can* learn to mix on cheaper turntables – all it takes is practice. **Dean Evans**, a drum'n'bass/hip-hop DJ remembers when he upgraded from Sound LAB belt-driven decks to Technics direct-drive: *'It was an amazing experience just to take them out of the box! The needle doesn't jump when you move the record back and forth, but then you start to mix – I had never used*

direct-drive before – and you've gotta learn all over again! You can get really cheap direct-drives now, but then you couldn't.'

So, readers, from that little story, I am sure you will agree that direct-drives are the way forward. You will find as you upgrade and eventually get a higher quality set of decks that you will have to perfect your mixing skills all over again for a few weeks because you don't have to compensate for lack of torque any more and that will take getting used to. More about that in chapter three ...

what make, how much?

A-ha! Take a deep breath, because this is where you have to give up going out for the rest of your life! Just kidding, but seriously, decks can be expensive and you will probably have to save up for them, or request them as your Christmas and birthday presents for the next couple of years.

There are quite a few decent direct-drives on the market at the moment, as well as things called starter kits, which have a mixer, headphones and all the necessary leads plus two decks. We went to DJ Leon of Flex FM, a pirate radio station, for some advice.

Leon also works at Kingston Sound and Light, a DJ equipment store. He thinks that if you are a beginner, the starter kits are great. Of course, the torque isn't

going to be as good as on more e)
but you don't want to spend all
something you might abandon after si
get bored (probably won't happen, bu
be sure). **Miss Behavin'**, a top female ~~ ~~, ~~ ~~. *I practised on a mate's decks for a couple of months to see if I was any good before I rushed out and bought a load of equipment that I might not have used!'*

There are starter kits made by Gemini, Numark or Kam for about £200 – but at this price some of them are going to be belt-driven, though Numark do a starter pack with direct-drives in this price range – so look out for special offers. The best starter pack to watch out for if you don't even have a stereo to plug your mixer into is Numark's DJ in a Box – it comes with everything you'd expect, but also a set of powered speakers with built-in amps, so you are ready to rock from the start.

Leon offers these sage words: *'It's better to start out with better decks and not such a good mixer. If you get really flimsy decks when you're starting out, you don't really learn too well on them. You need something a bit more solid. So get the best decks you can buy. You can learn all the flashy stuff with the mixer later on down the line. Also, all decks come with leads and anything that doesn't I'd give a wide berth to because they're trying to rip you off.'*

It seems that all the main names – Vestax, Gemini,

, Kam, Citronic, Numark – all have a budget ct-drive deck in their range and, at the moment, they are all hovering around £300–£400 a pair. And there are starter packs for £300–£350 that will be direct-drive. So don't go thinking it's got to be Technics or nothing. You *have* to make it as cheap as possible to start with and much later, when you are accomplished, then you can get a better set-up. If you are wondering why there aren't any specific models mentioned here, it's because a new deck is launched practically every month, so the only thing worth mentioning are the brands to look out for. Same goes for mixers.

where from?

As for where to get your gear, you need to check out the *Yellow Pages* because nowadays, it does seem that there is a DJ equipment shop in every town, or a hire place at least (that usually sells stuff too). You really should try before you buy, but this sometimes isn't possible if you live in the middle of nowhere. Major dealers are advertised in the back of music and DJ magazines. They highlight special offers and most of them do mail order and next-day delivery. Look out for reviews of mixers and decks in these magazines to help you decide – they are always very good and unbiased and if you can't get to a shop, buying over the phone or on the Net could be the answer. These web sites might come in useful: www.i-dj.co.uk, www.htfr.com. Again, music and DJ magazines will have details of other stores and web sites. BUT, if you live anywhere near a town with a Virgin Megastore or an HMV, they sell the starter packs too, so check them out.

Not all the major stores are based in the south of England – for example, Hard to Find Records (tel: 0121 687 7777), see the web site above, is based in Birmingham. Some of the bigger dealers will do a financial package whereby you beg the parents/rest of family/dog to buy it and you will make the monthly payments from your Saturday job/paper round/chimney sweeping. BUT, if you decide to go second-hand, you have to know what you're looking for – you can get Technics or Vestax at a lower price second-hand, but it isn't worth going for really cheap decks. This is because it is likely that the previous owner will have used them to learn on and will have thrashed the life out of them, leaving them on their last legs. Also, because they are cheaper they won't be able to handle that level of abuse all over again from you!

The Number One Rule about buying second-hand: never ever buy anything unless you've had a good go on it first. Make sure the Stop/Start button works properly and bring some records with you to have a spin. Move the pitch fader up and down to test it still works and check for missing screws, headshells and the like. You might even want to take along your own needles so you can get a better idea if there is any dodgy wiring, etc. Always try and haggle too!

check me out!

Unless you grew up in a cave on top of a very high mountain without TV, radio, or the Net, then you probably don't need to look at this picture of a deck. But just on the off chance you are a mountain dweller, take a peek.

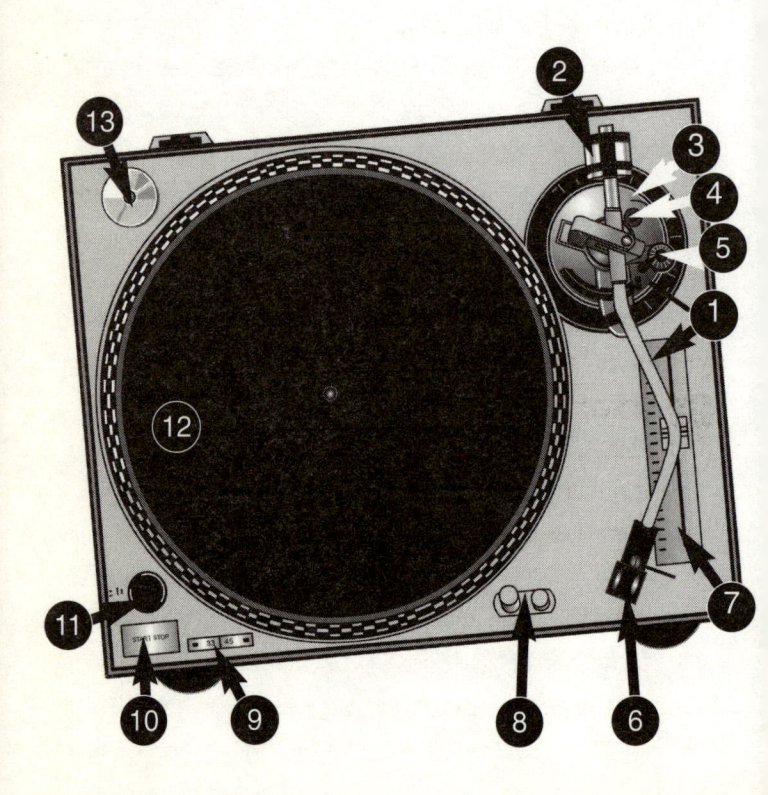

(1) **tone arm** You will need to set this up. More on that in a bit.

(2) **tone-arm weight** This balances the arm.

(3) **height ring** Twist this round to adjust the tone-arm height.

(4) **lock lever** This holds the height ring in place.

(5) **anti-skate dial** Turn this to adjust the swing of the arm.

(6) **headshell** Attach the cartridge here.

(7) **pitch slider** By moving this up and down, you can change the pitch (tone) and speed of a record by –8% to +8%. Too high and the vocals will sound like chipmunks! Some Vestax decks have a pitch bend facility which allows faster beats per minute, but keeps the original pitch intact so vocals don't sound hideous.

(8) **light** This allows you to see the grooves in the dark!

(9) **33/45 buttons** Allows you to select rpm.

(10) **start/stop button** Starts and stops the platter from spinning.

(11) **on/off switch** Bit obvious.

(12) **platter** Always use a slipmat.

(13) **platter weight** Put on the top of your records to keep them steady or put in the middle of seven inches without the centre part.

Before you do anything, read the instructions that come with your decks because they might tell you stuff you really didn't know.

how to set your tone arm

You can adjust this to suit yourself – whatever you feel comfortable with. If you twist the height ring the whole tone arm can be raised or lowered. The height of this can depend on what cartridge (or 'cart', which holds the stylus/needle) you use. Some people like to have the arm really high so that they have maximum down pressure on the needle – fiddle with it and see how you want to set it. When you've decided how to set it, lock it in position and – hey presto – almost ready to spin.

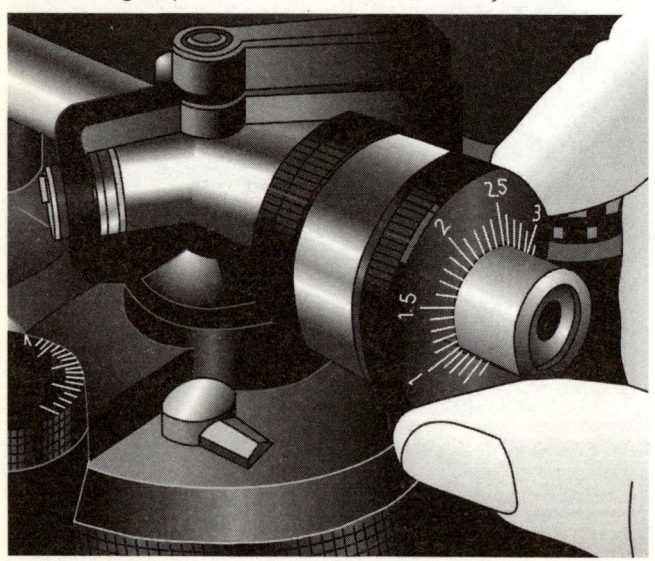

With the arm locked in place, it's time to set the weight, which balances the whole thing and affects how much weight is put on the cartridge. The instructions that come with your decks offer different advice, but these wise words come from the Plagia-wrists, a group of UK turntablists who you will hear more of in chapter four. They think the best way to set your counterweight is to actually pull the whole weight off and turn it round, so the calibrations (numbers) are facing away from the decks.

Next, slide the weight back on, pushing it as far forwards as possible so that more down force is applied to the needle at the front. Check the weight of your cartridge to see how much offset you will need to apply with the newly positioned counterweight.

Now you'll need to set the anti-skating. This controls how much the tone arm swings towards the centre of the deck. Again, the Plagia-wrists suggest just leaving the setting at '0' and this is fine for mixing and scratching alike.

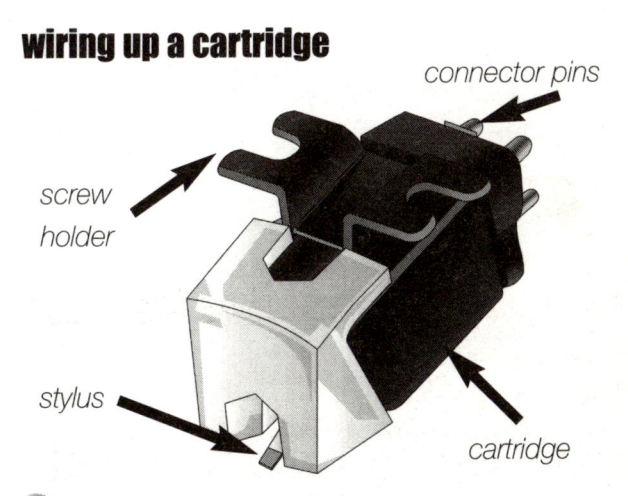

wiring up a cartridge

connector pins

screw holder

stylus

cartridge

When you buy your decks, they should come with cartridges (including a stylus, unless the shop is being stingy), but you can buy all sorts of cartridges and styli for your decks. The Stanton 500 ALII (around £30 each) are pretty standard and ideal for bedroom DJs and clubs alike and come with a stylus. There are obviously lots of carts out there ideal for scratching: Ortofon, Stanton, Numark and Shure are makes to look out for, with Shure being the make that the Plagia-wrists use for scratching, but you could make do with the standard Stanton ones. As **DJ Leon** points out, *'A lot of people think you have to put a lot of weight on the needle, but you just have to have the tone arm adjusted properly.'*

Cartridges (including stylus) can range from £12 each to a jaw-droppingly expensive £200 a pair! And replacement needles can be as cheap as £12 each to not so cheap £60 each. Obviously there is no need for you to have the expensive stuff – the cheaper end of the scale is OK for starting out. If you can afford to, don't go for stuff at the very bottom of the scale, only because they might carve your records up more quickly.

You may have heard about spherical and elliptical needles. Most needles are spherical and these are the ones you need for all DJing, including scratching. Elliptical needles are used on good-quality hi-fis and cost a lot more, but the sound is much better, However, they do carve up your vinyl more quickly.

You *can* also buy cartridges that don't need wiring up; Prime Cuts from the Scratch Perverts recommends a Numark CX1000. All you do is plug it into the tone arm – nothing else required. But if you need to know how to wire up, take a look here …

● Unscrew the headshell from the tone arm with a jeweller's screwdriver. The idea is to attach the wires from the headshell on to the connector pins coming out of the cart. You will notice that the wires are colour-coded, so you just attach red to red, blue to blue, etc. You must be very careful when doing this as the wire can break if handled clumsily.

● Prise open the silver clamp-style grips on the end of the wires with a pair of tweezers. This will allow you to slip them on to the connector pins easily and when attached, you can gently close the grips with pliers around the pin. See our helpul diagram below.

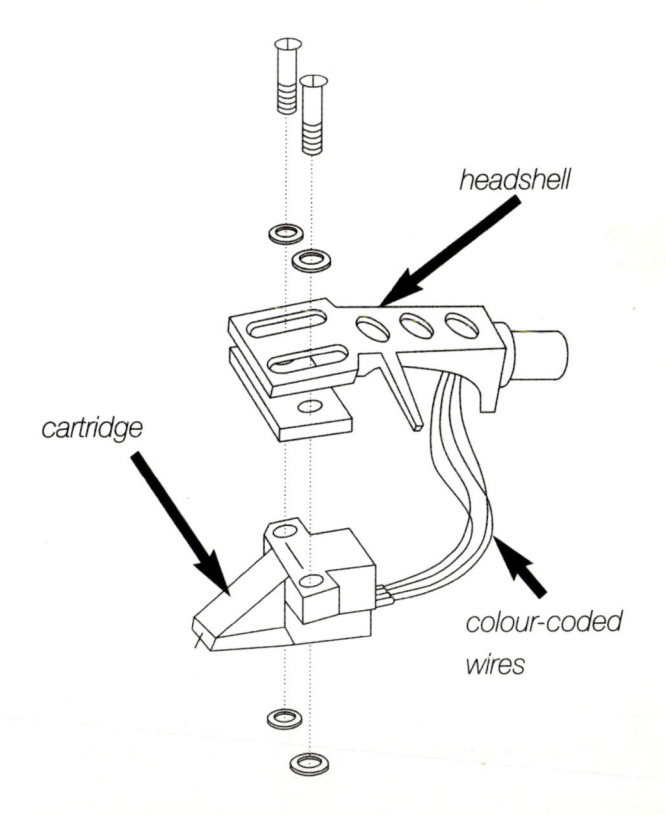

To keep the weight in place, slide the screw holder (looks like a pair of wings) directly on to the top of the cart. The screws need this to have something to go into.

● Put the weight on top of the screw holder (the weight will place more down force on the needle), and then align the holes on the weight with the holes on the screw holder.

● Screw the weight, screw holder and cart to the headshell. Position the cart as far forwards as possible for stability, using the grooves on the underneath of the headshell as a guide.

● Now you can attach the headshell and cart to the tone arm. Slide it in and then twist the tightener as far as it will go. It shouldn't move once you have attached it or the cart will wobble in the record's grooves!

● If you want to scratch, having a straight tone arm is a lot better because it keeps the needle in the groove of the record much more securely than a curved one. If you don't have a straight tone arm, fix the cartridge at an angle in the headshell so that it's aligned with the counterweight, copying the straight arm.

mixing it up

When you buy your mixer always read the manual because, unlike decks, some mixers vary a lot and have added extras, and you want to know what they're for, don't you?

1) power!

2) crossfader By sliding this across, you move the

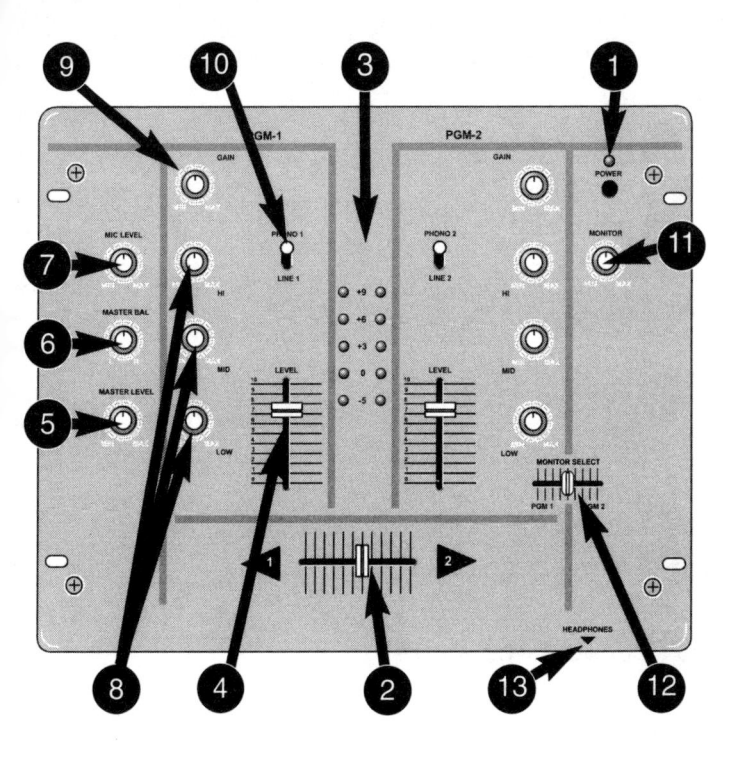

output from channel one (deck A) to channel two (deck B).

③ led (light-emitting diode) meter Shows the level of each channel, or the master output, in red flashing lights. This means you can check the loudness of one track against the other and even up the levels by fiddling with the gains/trim control.

④ channel volume slider Allows you to control the volume of just a single channel.

⑤ master level This is the overall volume regardless of other volume controls on the mixer.

⑥ master balance Decides which speaker the

➤ 43 ◀

sound comes out of – keep in the middle for both left and right.

(7) mic level Adjusts volume level on the mic.

(8) eq selection These adjust high, mid and low EQ.

(9) gain/trim This finely tunes the channel volume by boosting the incoming signal from the deck/CD player. Do not mistake it for the volume – that is the master.

(10) input selector Selects the input source to the channel – basically whether you are using decks or a CD player.

(11) monitor Turn this to alter the headphone volume.

(12) monitor select You can choose which channel you want to hear in the headphones, or hear both.

(13) headphone socket

Time to decide which mixer you want for which type of music you are spinning. If you are playing house/garage/drum'n'bass/techno/trance or any of the other million genres of dance music, then you should go for a simple mixer that doesn't look too much like a flight deck. According to **DJ Leon**, *'They are all a much of a muchness. It is all down to personal preference.'* He's right – there are so many mixers out there that it is impossible to recommend a particular model for a beginner because, as we mentioned earlier, there is a new one coming out every month. It would take up the whole book to go through them all and we've got more important things on our mind …

Basically, all you need is a two-channel mixer with a crossfader and maybe some EQs (they really aren't necessary), two-channel volume faders, an LED meter, headphone volume control and master volume – just check the diagram to see what's what. There are other things you need, which are quite standard, but you can look at them on the diagram.

The EQs on your mixer control the different frequencies on a record. There's bass/low (bass drum), mid-range (vocals) and treble/high (high hats, cymbals). Some mixers will only have bass and treble. By playing with these dials/faders, you can really change the sound of tracks and blend them together seamlessly – more on that in the next chapter.

What you do need to know is that the crossfader won't last forever. All crossfaders are replaceable and cost in the region of £30 for one at the cheaper end of the market. If you are a scratch DJ, your fader will pack up even more quickly because you will be bashing the life out of it.

Makes to look out for are Gemini, Numark, Stanton, Kam, Vestax, Citronic – all have mixers at the beginners' end of the market. Prices vary from under £100 to under £1,000 (ooh, I'll have two please …) You will pick up a decent bedroom mixer for under £150 but, of course, there is always the second-hand option – again, don't forget to have a go on it and look out for wear and tear.

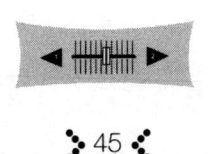

to scratch or not to scratch

If you want to be a scratch DJ then you need a mixer with crossfader curve adjust and crossfader reverse switch (or hamster switch, so-called because a turntablist crew called the Bullet-Proof Hamsters invented it). These are necessary for coming up with those cheeky scratches. Scratch mixers look similar to other mixers except they tend to have all the EQs and other buttons at the top so that they are out of the way. Sometimes they can be a lot narrower and have only a low and a high EQ. The curve adjust and hamster switches can be either on the top of the mixer with all the other flashing lights and buttons, or underneath at the front.

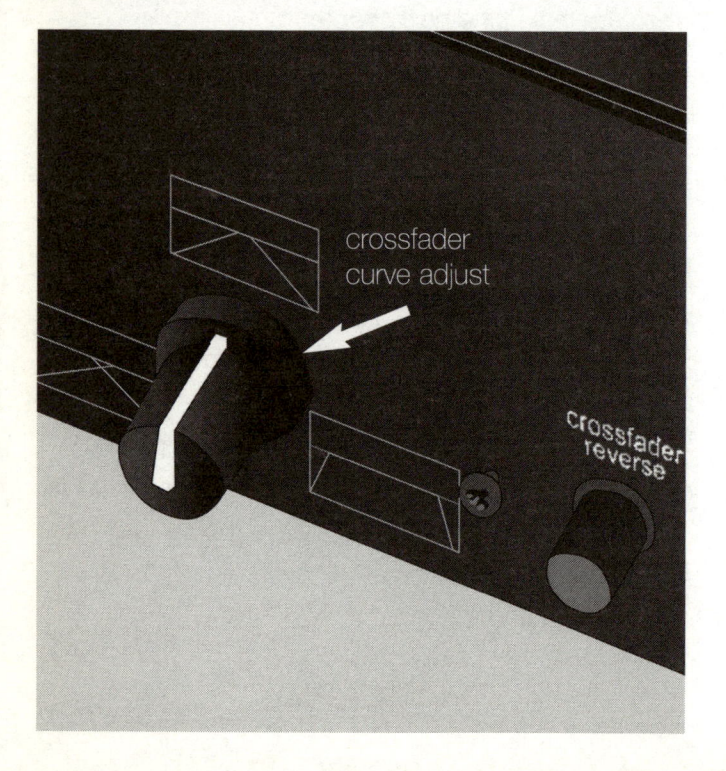

The curve adjust changes the smoothness of the fader as you slide it from one channel to another. If you are mixing house or garage, you want the transition from one channel to the other to be very gradual so that both channels blend seamlessly (assuming you are a great mixer, that is!) When you're scratching, you need the crossfader to have a cutting point so that you can have a sharper sound for better scratch definition. So you switch the fader to a sharper shelving curve. Check out the pic so you know what to look for on a mixer.

The hamster switch changes the channel output on the crossfader. You might be sliding the fader from channel one (deck A) to channel two (deck B), but flick the switch and channel one becomes deck B and channel two becomes deck A. This and everything else to do with scratching will be explained fully in chapter four.

getting set up

In order to start treading the path to greatness, you'll have to plug in all your gear and get wired. It is quite simple. If you have a stereo, you can plug it all into its amp. The diagram over the page will help you get the wires in the right place. Check your manual too because they always have assembly instructions. All leads have a left and a right plug – just so you know! It's always a nightmare the first time.

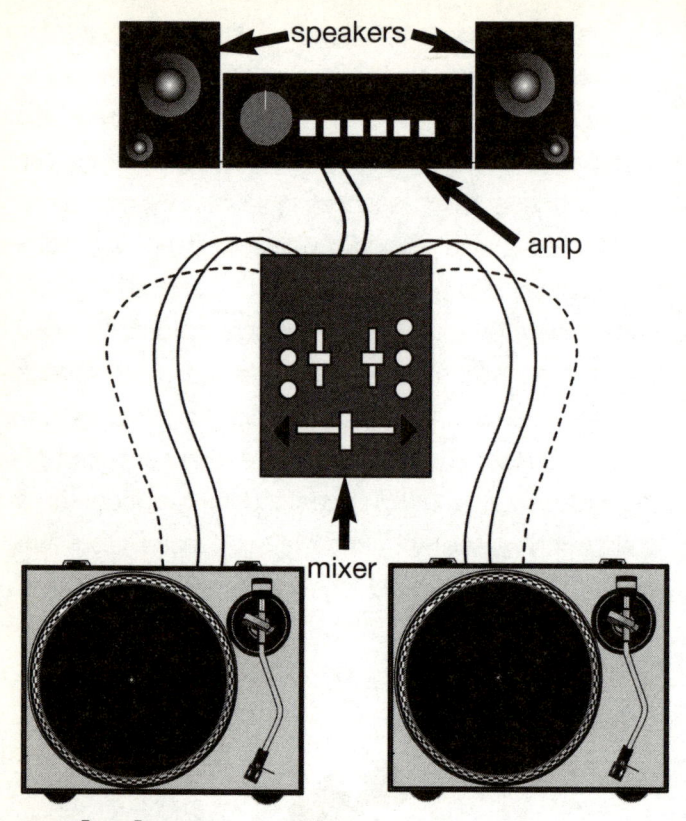

need to know

🎵 You should remember when wiring up that the output of your turntables is a phono signal and must go into the phono inputs on your mixer. All outputs on your mixer will be line level and can be called master out, line out or booth out.

🎵 If you plug a line signal into the phono input on your amp you will blow the amp because it will be too loud (as the mixer has already amplified it). The phono input amplifies the sound from your record player on your stereo. So you connect the master out into the aux input in your stereo, or you can use the CD inputs.

● The earth or ground lug at the back of the mixer is where you attach the earth cable from your decks to avoid signal hum.

● If you want to do a mix tape, plug in your cassette deck (or Mini Disc player etc.) to the record outputs/playback connectors.

● If you want to use CD players, just plug the CD decks into the line inputs for channel one and two on the mixer. It doesn't matter if you only have a two-channel mixer, because if you look on the mixer pic on page 43, you will see the input selector switches. When you are playing vinyl, you will have them switched to phono, but when you want to play a CD, flick to line, so you can have four decks for the price of two! Don't forget to switch back when you play vinyl again on the same channel or nothing will come out.

● Always switch on your turntables or CD decks first, then your mixer, and finally your amp. When you turn off, reverse the order, switching off the amp first, then the mixer and finally the decks.

then there were cd decks...

CD decks are big business now. In the last few years there have been lots of advances in CD-deck manufacturing. Some of them even allow you to scratch and make sounds just like vinyl. Makes to look for are Pioneer, Denon, Stanton, Gemini and Numark. It is impossible to go into this in great depth as CD decks are all different and, with technology moving so fast, by the time this book comes out, another new invention will have been made. However, the Pioneer CDJ1000 is amazing if you live in La La Land and are a millionaire. It has a massive jog wheel that makes cueing up and adjusting the pitch mid-mix really easy and lots of FX, like internal memory (you can make a loop and save it to use later) and instant reverse. BUT, it is humungously expensive and not likely to come down in price in the near future – it can cost around £800 for one deck! Excuse me while I choke on a crumb ...

Everyone I have talked to is using CDs now as part of their sets and if you have a whole back catalogue of tunes on CD and feel it is more your medium, then maybe you should think about getting a dual deck set-up.

There are two types of CD decks: rack-mount and desktop. You can get desktop dual set-ups and single ones, but the rack-mount have two CD players as standard. The single ones tend to be more expensive. Rack-mount are easier to transport, take up less space, and the more expensive ones have the same effects as decent desktops – such as pitch bend, which allows you to speed up records using the pitch control, but keep the tone at the original pitch, so there won't be any chipmunks. And anti-shock – if a CD jumps, the machine will carry on playing it from a six- to fifteen-second memory buffer until you sort it, or the memory ends. They also load from the front and slide out like a normal CD player. You can't use them on a flat surface – they have to be on a shelf above the mixer, or down below. But beware, when you press that eject button, you'll get knocked on the knees, or somewhere more painful!

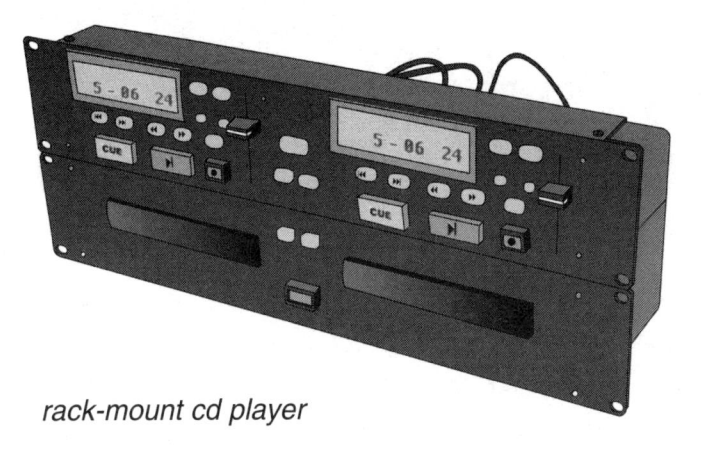

rack-mount cd player

Desktops take up more space and are not as easy to carry, but they nearly always have extra features, like the Pioneer CDJ 1000, and extra features are certainly what the more accomplished DJ will look for. Most of these are top-loading too, which means quicker access for whipping out a CD and placing in another, though some have trays that slide out from the front.

'Go into a shop and badger the staff to let you have a go on different models. For beginners, Gemini do some cheap double ones,' reckons **DJ Leon**. See what you feel

desktop cd player

comfortable with and what you can afford.

There are machines called MP3 mixers now that you can use to download tracks straight from the Net and play out that night, but we are stepping into Star Trek territory and, right now, all you need to know about them is that they exist.

headphones

The average cost of a pair of decent headphones is from around £40 up to about £100. Of course there are always going to be those ones that cost the same as a second-hand car, but you don't need to know about them. Good headphone makes are Sennheiser, Sony, Stanton, Beyer, Denon and Technics. To start with, DJ Leon says you should get closed-back ones because they are easier to hear if you have your system up loud. Also, make sure they are comfortable and not too heavy. You don't want a headache after a couple of hours' practice. You should also be able to wear them one ear on, one ear off.

If you are going to venture into a club and play to a crowd, then you really need to spend a bit more money than you would otherwise – sometimes your headphones are your only ticket to actually being able to hear how the mix is going while all around you is a madhouse. And this means you will need to look for certain attributes:

Wide-frequency response – this means the headphones can handle frequencies as low as sub-bass through to the highest notes that only dogs can hear! Measured in decibels.

High sound pressure level – this is how loud

they will go before they blow up! This is also measured in decibels. A test of how good the headphones are is to turn them up to the highest volume and if you still have good sound quality – buy them!

Impedance – this is way too technical and geeky and will start to sound like a science lesson, so all you need to know is the lower the impedance, the higher you can push the volume. It will say on them if it is low or not.

Having said that, a really good pair will still not be tooooo expensive – between £100 and £150.

slipmats

If your decks come with those 'big biscuits' as the Plagia-wrists call chunky slipmats, bin them! You want nice thin ones, preferably ones that don't have a load of print on them because they will rub off on to your records and look duff. If you are scratching, you want as much slippiness as possible. The Plagia-wrists say that they use the plastic inside covers of twelve inchers and cut them to size, pop them over the spindle on the platter and then put the slipmat on top of that. It's like it's been buttered! You can use greaseproof paper too.

That's it on the hardware. There are a million upgrades you can do for your set-up, but all you need to know at the moment is the basics. Maybe in a year's time or even less than that, you can start looking for bigger and better gear, but till then, you have to master what you've got and decide what you're going to play.

chapter three

it's all in the mix

“Because I didn't own decks that you could mix on at home, I guess you can say I learned as I was playing out” – graham gold

four to the floor

In the first chapter, you will have heard the terms 'four to the floor' or 'four-bar beat'. This refers to the structure of nearly all dance music. If you listen to your records, most genres have the four-bar beat (though there are exceptions and there will be in everything to do with DJing!) Count one, two, three, four as you listen to the record from the beginning. If you have any sort of ear for music, you will instantly hear where the start of the bar is and should be able to pick it up even if you plonk the needle in the middle of the track. Something you can't teach is how to tell where the beginning of the bar is – it is instinctive and will make learning to mix much harder than it already is if you don't know.

So dance tracks are made up of four-bar beats, it also means they can be made up of multiple phrases of four: eight, sixteen and thirty-two (most records are in bars of eight or sixteen). To cut to the basics, the four/four beat is used to build up the track from the intro, which will be a stripped-down version of the main tune kicking off with the bass drum. Next comes the full version of the tune, which is normally several bars looped together in bars of eight or sixteen. Sometimes there will be a break in this, but the break that is really important is the one that builds up to the climax – the part of the record where you will get that tingling feeling and the crowd/your mates in the bedroom go wild. Really, you shouldn't mix into a build-up of a tune, but there are exceptions of course. After the climax, the tune winds down and usually slips back to a bare bones version again, rather like the intro.

If you need a typical record, *Energy 52* by Café Del Mar is a classic example of intro, full version, build-up, climax and come down. It is really hard to explain the beat structure of a tune and the only way you can hear what I am saying is if you listen to your records. Count the beats and really listen to the theme – how is the track put together and what quantity of four/four does it rely on for the main tune? Eight bars, sixteen bars?

So now you have a (very) basic knowledge of how tunes are hung together, shall we proceed with the mixing?

beat matching

There is no wrong or right way to learn this; everyone has their own way and this is mine, handed down to me by Mr Benn, the best bedroom DJ ever. Also, I might have asked a few top DJs for some of their hot tips too, and you should take heed – they are the ones out there playing to massive crowds week in, week out.

So, what is beat matching? It is the ability to make two tunes, one on each deck, both run in sync with the same beats per minute (tempo/speed). The idea is to be able to blend one into the other seamlessly without there being a change in the beat. Sounds easy, right? Well, cueing isn't so hard and will only take a matter of hours to get to grips with. As for the rest …

cueing a tune

Karl 'Tuff Enuff' Brown suggests starting with two copies of the same record – so go and buy them. Something with a very easy to hear four/four beat and not too many complicated frilly extras that will confuse you. Remember, mix with what you actually like playing. Just because UK garage is missing two beats, doesn't mean you shouldn't learn with it – it still kicks off with a drum beat at the start of the bar, so use that as your starting

point. It is more vocal-orientated and doesn't tend to have big drum rolls, climaxes and build-ups like four/four tunes. As **Karl** says about two step: ***'You just have to know your beat and bar combination, and where the instrumental breaks are ... It doesn't matter if you've practised enough.'***
Again, some DJs think learning with drum'n'bass would be too hard, but D & B DJ **Dean Evans** disagrees: ***'Drum'n'bass is the easiest to mix because it is quite broken down. The elements of the track are a bit with drums, a bit with drums and bass, then a break down, then the drums on their own, then the bass – it's all very cut up, so when you're mixing it, you can flip between the two.'***

let the lesson begin

Plug in your headphones. Have the same copies on each deck and have the crossfader set so channel one/record A is open. Set the pitch slider at '0' on both decks. '0' is usually a no no, as the slider can get stuck in the groove (listen for the click and you will see), making small adjustments either side of '0' really tricky. However, the point of this is so you know both records are at the same speed. Start record A, which will be channel one on the mixer, and let it play.

Put your headphones on – one ear on, one ear off

for now (so you can hear one tune in the headphones and the one that is playing) and set the levels – not too loud, but loud enough so you can hear it against the speakers from your stereo. I will mention split-level cueing for headphones in a bit – not all mixers have it, and the chances are, yours won't. Press the cue button above the channel two fader – this will allow you to hear record B on the other deck in your headphones.

To cue up record B, put the needle on at the beginning and let it play – you will only hear it in your headphones – now put your finger on the record and wind it backwards until you pass that first beat again. Hold the record there and rock it backwards and forwards over the beat, so you get the feel of where the beginning of the beat is. Continue rocking the first beat in time with the record that's live and count – one, two, three, four.

How to tell when to release the record is difficult at first, so how about a tip from **Paul Oakenfold**? He passed on this bit of advice to Lisa Loud when she was learning to DJ: *'**Every single four-to-the-floor record is made on the premise of bars of eight, so a record will go one, two, three, four, five, six, seven, eight. Now, if you count your way through a record like that, start to finish on a bass kick, then every time a change in the record happens – i.e. a vocal is introduced, something musical happens, or there's gonna be a change in**

the rhythm – it will happen on bar one after bar eight. That's when you release your other record. That's the best tip I've ever had!' – **Lisa Loud**. Generally this is true; if anything happens, it happens on the first beat of a bar, whether it is eight or sixteen. Keep those ears flapping.

So when the live record is coming up to the last beat of a bar, you will be counting one, two, three, four, five, six, seven, eight, go, and on 'go' release the record. You may well get it first time (a genius, obviously) and have both tunes perfectly matched so you can slide the fader into the middle on Open with both tracks playing seamlessly together over the speakers as one – and then again you might not. More likely, you will have let go too early or too late. Keep rewinding record B with your finger and having another go until you get the hang of it.

If you have belt-driven decks, you will always have this problem of the records not letting go at the right speed because the torque (motor) isn't strong enough and will slow down the platter when it is stopped manually. To get round this, you need to throw record B into the mix by giving it a little push. How much you will have to throw it is something only you will know after you have practised.

To correct too slow or too fast release, you can manipulate the vinyl with your fingers. If you have started too early and the beat is ahead, put your finger on the side of the platter (where the bumps are) very gently and slow the record down until the beats are in

slowing down a record

sync again. If you have let go too late and the beat is behind, press your index finger on the record label and gently move the record round, speeding it up slightly so it catches up and the beats match. Each time, when the beats match, slide the fader to the middle so you can hear both records as one.

speeding up a record

DJ Leon said he couldn't even cue up a record when he began: *'I didn't have a clue. We used to go out clubbing and listen to the DJs and didn't know where one tune started and the other began, and we thought – ah, they're gods, we wanna do that! So we'd go home and try and figure it out. That's the long way round of doing it!'*

changing pitch

This is the hardest part of beat matching and the point at which a lot of people sell their decks for a computer or a bike. The two Ps are in play again: Persistence and Practice.

Now you can cue a record and get the first beat to match, you need to be able to get records to play at the same tempo/beats per minute/pitch. Still with the same two records, set record A at +3% and keep record B at '0'.

As before, listen to record A with your ears and listen to record B in the headphones. Cue up record B and let it go at the beginning of a bar on record A. Hear how it is in sync for about two beats, slide the fader into the middle and then hear a herd of buffalo crash into your room! Record B is too slow.

Because we are using two copies of the same record, you will know where to move the pitch control on record B, so try it at 3% as well. See how the two records stay in time for a bit and then slowly drift out of sync. This is because the percentages aren't exact on each deck – not fair, is it? It can vary by a few points of a percent on every one.

Now you will really have to use your ears. Is record B too fast or too slow? When both tracks are in time, you will just hear the bass pounding 'boom'. But if the cued record is too slow, you might be able to distinguish a 'd-boom' or if the cued record is too fast, it'll sound like 'b-doom'. BUT, you will only be able to hear this fine difference after an age of practising. To know exactly what you should be listening for in your headphones, play record A and B in time and then slow down/speed up record B to get a feel for how that sounds. However, you will have to do this with two different records, or you will experience something called 'phasing'. More on that later.

Until you really can tell the difference, you will have to make guesses, either starting again and resetting the pitch or speeding the record up or down with your fingers and adjusting the pitch control accordingly to match. Also, if you rest it and start again and the beats seem to gallop off even more quickly, it means you have set the pitch too fast and you need to take it back to the original setting and then back a tiny bit more.

Try moving the pitch up and down on the scale on both decks from +8 to –8 without looking at where you have moved the pitch slider to and use your ears to make record B's pitch match record A's. This is hard enough with two records that are the same, but you really need to try and do it with two different ones as well. You will want to smash those two copies by now I would have thought …

mixing different tunes!

Two different records means different BPMs (beats per minute) – argh! The tune will be different, everything will be different – how do you feel about that? No more safety nets with the same two records – time for the real challenge. You will still be cueing up on the first beat of a bar and releasing on the first beat of a bar, but this time you will have to listen more carefully.

What you have to look out for now is the volume of the tracks. This is where the gain control comes in (assuming you have one on your mixer). For playing the same tunes, you will have had it set in the middle of the dial, now it could be moved either way. Each channel has a gains control and it measures the output from each deck coming into the mixer and then going out again into the amp and through the speakers. Think of this as measuring the loudness of each particular vinyl pressing on each deck – and you will realize that it can vary.

The idea is to have the incoming record set at the same volume as the record that is playing or it will overpower it and sound diabolical! You can check levels by looking at the LED meter, the row of lights that are next to the EQs (assuming you have those too!) for each channel. They are numbered −30 db (decibels), then −25, −15, −10, −6, −3, 0, +3 and ending in +6. You might need to adjust record A so that it peaks between 0 and +3. You test this by putting the needle on in the main part of the tune, when it is going to be banging out the loudest and set the gains accordingly till the lights flicker in-between those points. Do the same with record B in your headphones, testing the levels at the main section of the tune. Once you have both records peaking at the same point, record B is ready to be cued.

BUT – what if you don't have a gains control? Some very basic mixers won't have them. **DJ Leon** has this advice: *'Use the channel faders instead. Have the volume on each channel about two-thirds of the way up the slider, then you can walk it up if you are playing a twelve-inch next to an album, or a quiet pressing.'* You will need to listen as you bring the tune in and assess whether you need to boot it up a bit.

So, you release record B and it is in time for about three seconds and then goes out again! Calm down, no one said it was going to be easy; at least the volumes are equal! This is where you hone your skills, getting the beats to match by using a mixture of speeding and slowing down the record and slowly moving the pitch slider up and down to match what you have just done with your fingers on the vinyl. Eventually it will happen, but if you are maniacally sliding the pitch fader up and down, and one minute it is too fast, the next too slow, it means the changes you are making are too big – be calm and make smaller adjustments.

Also, take a break if you feel a bit like throwing things – five minutes in the fresh air always manages to focus you. There is nothing else to say except practise, practise, practise. As producer and DJ **Bob Bhamra** says: ***'When you buy decks, you don't go out for the first year, but then it eventually clicks.'***

If you have a friend who is learning at the same time, you can play together: you put one record on and then they put a record on and you have to mix into each other's records to stop the rot setting in. Also, you get to play with different records from your own if you are not too well funded. It's also more fun – which is the main point, after all!

Every DJ has to work at it – beat mixing isn't an instant skill, though some people find it easier than others. **DJ Wes** from award-winning shop Plastic Fantastic Records remembers his slog on the decks: ***'I was cueing up records and letting them go at the right time, but couldn't keep them in the mix. Beat mixing only comes with practice. It took me nine months to get happy with it and I was on the headphones every night!'***

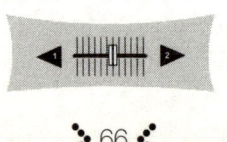

headphones or no headphones

So far, all we have looked at is mixing with one ear on and one ear off, or single ear monitoring. But it is good to know other ways of listening to your records and mixing them too. Just listening in your headphones is a useful trick to learn and will stand you in good stead in the future for club DJing. You really need a mixer with a headphone split and blend button to be able to mix in the phones. The split button allows you to hear the live track in one ear and the cued track in the other so that you can hear the beats separately and are able to tell if they are in sync or not.

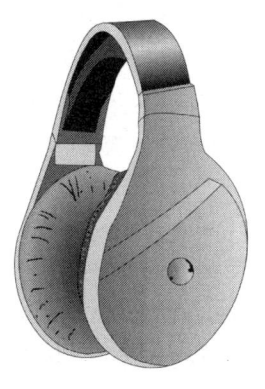

However, some people find this confusing and prefer to have the button pressed to blend, so you can hear both tunes in both ears, as you would if you weren't wearing any headphones, and mix that way. You have to work out what works best for you and fiddle with the volume of each tune. Judge Jules' top mixing tip is not to have your headphones too loud. Ear damage is something that you can't ever recover from!

DJ Paulette reckons it is good to learn without

headphones too: ***'I was told to start doing that because it gives you an idea of what you're listening to. If you play two records both at the wrong speed at full volume, it sounds yuk. But you get a feel for slowing this one down and that one up without doing it in your headphones. If, heaven forbid, the monitor packs up (in a club) or the headphones don't work, you know that within two bars you can get those records to match. It covers you!'***

Try it in the bedroom at home. Switch both decks on and have record A playing out over the stereo and then start record B. Listen to the hi-hats, cymbals and bass resonating off the turntable, rather like listening to someone else's personal stereo turned up annoyingly high! You can mix the first beat of record B into record A without listening in the phones and hear if it is in time. Slide the fader across and make any extra adjustments as you listen to record B come into the mix. This wouldn't work in a club where the music was so loud you couldn't hear anything other than the track playing over the PA. In that case, as DJ Paulette said, you will be playing both records at once and adjusting the speed of the incoming record live and hopefully getting it within two bars. Phew! Scary stuff.

it's more than matching beats ...

You will be practising and getting on your decks every spare second you have by now, trying to beat match perfectly so you can leave the tunes in the mix, go off and grab some food, come back and find them still in the mix without having wandered off into galloping horses. But it isn't just about sliding the fader across the minute the tunes are in sync in the headphones.

Producer and DJ **Bob Bhamra** tells the truth: *'I'm very precise when it comes to producing and that's what I'm like when I mix, so I like to think of it in terms of the structure of the song. Some people just wanna mix and go "That's in time, those two beats match." Yes, it's in time but the pitch is wrong, or you're playing a chorus, this song's building up for a chorus and you've mixed a song over it! I like to have structure, hear the* *song and then come in at a good point.'*

As I said at the beginning of the chapter, generally, it is an unwritten rule that you shouldn't slide the fader across and mix into a build-up of a song, also, mixing vocals into vocals so they clash is another no no. Listen to what you are doing; think about where to bring in the incoming record. **St.John de Zilva** from DJ Workshop agrees: *'If you say you can beat mix, you have to (a) keep it in time and (b) do it in a way that makes musical sense ... Some kids have problems with knowing when to take the mix out ... I can't say that it's after twelve bars or something, it depends on what kind of music it is. Those are things you learn in time.'*

Knowing your records is a good way to get round this problem and the P word again – practise. Tape radio shows that have DJs mixing live on them and check out their mixes – how could you adapt anything you hear to your style? Listening to other DJs is good advice, but don't just copy them, be yourself. There is already a Sasha, an EZ, Stanton Warriors, Carl Cox – just use their sets/mix CDs as a point of reference. **DJ Paulette** recalls how she fell upon perfecting her mixing: *'I remember Graham Park giving me a cassette at a Southport Weekender and I just listened to it and listened to it. And it was like that, really, just hearing how others were doing it, but not wanting to be like them, but hearing how they did it and thinking, How can I apply* *that to what I want to play?'*

The best way to know how you are doing is to follow **Miss Behavin**'s self-improvement tip: ***'Record yourself as you practise. Then stop and re-listen to your mistakes; that way you can work out what went wrong and why and learn from it.'***

cool trickery*
***warning – advanced stuff!**

I am not going to go into *all* the extra stuff you can do because (a) you might not even have any EQs on your mixer and (b) it complements what knowledge you already have, and if you haven't perfected your beat matching, then this is pointless as it will only distract you from practising the basics! These simple tricks are only the tip of the iceberg of what is possible using the decks and a mixer to manipulate records and create something different.

eqs

If you are bringing in a track and there is nowhere for its thumping bass to fit in with the live track, you can avoid an overpowering bassline by turning down the low/bass frequency on the incoming track so you are just blending in the rest of the tune and producing a 'clean' mix. Then gradually drop out the bass line from the live track and at the same time blend in the bass from the incoming track. Simple, eh?

You can do the same with the other EQs. If cymbals or vocals are getting in the way of a mix, you can turn them down and make the mix smoother. Other tricks are filter effects, when you turn the mid and treble right down and then gradually bring them back into the mix. These tricks *can* make a great tune even better, but only a really competent DJ can work the EQs so that this really makes a difference. Too much EQ trickery can sound cluttered and may distract from how cool the original tune was in the first place …

other smart moves

For phasing you will need two copies of the same record – now where were those two records you bought? In the bin? Best get two more! Play both records in time, one on each deck. Slide the crossfader into the middle so they are both blasting out of the speakers and gently speed up or slow down one of the tunes. You will hear the record 'phase' between the two speakers – it sounds like 'whooshing'. Cool!

Preview a tiny section of a tune you will play later on. Find a few bars that are typical of that tune, get the speed roughly right (it only has to be synchronized for a few bars) and line it up on the first bar. Wait for a part in the live record where the cued record would sound cool, and then let it go and open the crossfader so you can hear it over the speakers. When it has played its two bars, close the fader so only the live track is playing and spin back the sample and repeat. This teases the crowd, especially when you finally mix in another record altogether.

 Backspinning a record can be quite effective, if done well. Record B is playing – put a finger on it and pull it right back so it spins and immediately slide the fader across for record A, which you will have let go of from its first bar, cutting off record B mid-spin. You have to practise this and watch out for warped records and dodgy needles, because it could make the tone arm jump all over the place and ruin the effect. You can also spin the record forwards too. Don't overdo it though – it is cool to use as a sample in the middle of a mix and as an 'if all else fails' tool, but is no replacement for getting in the mix.

 Another 'if all else fails' trick is to switch off the record that's playing using the On/Off switch – it will gradually slow down and slide the fader across to the incoming record.

 You can bring in the bass of the incoming record for a few beats by whipping the crossfader over from channel two to channel one and then back again so the existing track is playing again. You can play around with this, making new combinations.

cd mixing

This section is very brief because all CD players are so different and not all of them have special added extras. We are just going to touch on the basics of beat matching and a few effects so that you can go away and try it out for yourself on whatever set-up you have. You might be using a CD as a third deck or just mixing with CDs, but this will work for both options.

cueing

Put your CD in the tray and check your mixer's line/phono switch is flicked to line for the channel you are playing. You won't hear anything otherwise.

The crossfader should be slid all the way over so that the other deck (CD or vinyl) is playing live. Listen in your headphones and press Play, then wait for the first beat of the first bar. It could be at the beginning or after a little intro. When you've found it, press Pause as soon as you can after the beat.

Now use the jog wheel to find the beginning of the beat by turning it backwards. It should just be on the start of the beat rather than too far behind, or it will come in too late.

When you are sure you have found the exact point, press Cue – this will save the starting point. You can test if it is right by pressing Play – making sure it really is hot off its marks. Just press Cue to get back to your starting point. If you don't feel it is right, start again.

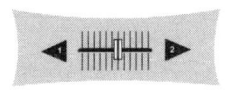

beat matching

With deck one playing live, you need to concentrate on that for a minute. As before, when we were talking about mixing vinyl, you need to listen to how the track is broken down. Is it in bars of eight or sixteen? Count from the start of a bar to find out and on the first beat of the new bar (remember, look out for a change in music, added vocals, that sort of thing), release the CD by pressing Play.

Listen very carefully in the headphones – are the tracks in time? If they sound like they are galloping ahead at the Grand National, the CD track is too fast. Move the pitch slider down and reduce the speed until the beats meet up. Now press Cue to get back to the start. Wait for the initial beat of another section and press Play.

If they are behind this time, move the pitch up until the beats join and then hit Cue and start again. Keep doing this until you feel the beats are matched and are confident enough to let your mix loose.

Now go back to the beginning and press Cue. Then, on the first beat of a new section, release your mix and slide the crossfader into the middle at a suitable point so that both tunes are playing through the speakers. The tracks may well stay in time, but more than likely you will have to adjust them slightly at first. Do this either by nudging ahead the incoming track, or slowing it down ever so slightly using the jog wheel.

You will find this a lot easier if you learned on vinyl, but, as usual, if not you will need to … PRACTISE! Argh! No getting away from it.

Don't forget, you will have to take on board all the previous info on not mixing in choruses, build-ups, vocals over vocals and finding the best place to bring in your mix – again, all down to experience.

a few simple tricks

To tease the crowd with a sample of a record you might play if they cheer enough, try this. Find an a cappella section (vocal only) on a CD, with no beats under it. You can buy a cappella CDs, but if you don't have any, a lot of intros on tunes start off with an a cappella vocal.

Find the section you want to use and cue it at the beginning – make sure the cue is accurate, with no delay whatsoever! Next, in the headphones, get it in time with the live track. When you are happy with it, hit Cue.

Move the crossfader into the middle and when you come to a bit in the live track where it would be ideal to throw in your sample, wait for the beginning of a bar and hold down the Cue button instead of Play. Hold it for as long as you want the sample to play. The minute you stop, the sample will stop playing and revert back to the cue point. Nice one! Mess around and do all sort of combinations – you can shoot the whole sample, or just one word.

There are other tricks, like FX and looping, but these are not all available on every CD deck. You can work out new ideas just by messing around with what you already have and when you are more confident and ready to go one step further, upgrade to better equipment.

what the pros say about mixing

Of course, you will make up stuff yourself as you improve, but don't be thinking that mixing and trickery are all there is to DJing. **Judge Jules** says: *'I think technically amazing DJs can often lack "presence" behind the decks, which is arguably more important.'* Drum'n'bass/hip-hop DJ **Dean Evans** agrees, *'It doesn't matter about mixing, it just depends on what level you want to get to. If every single tune you put on rocks, then it doesn't matter.'* **Ali B** has the same thought: *'I think it's really important to point out that mixing is not the most important side of DJing, and I'd hate to put people off if they were not as technically good as they should be. I definitely think the most important things are the records. Mixing is just so secondary.'* Remember these quotes when you keep comparing yourself to some technically brilliant wizard, thinking you will never be that good.

There are other factors that make up a DJ, as **St.John de Zilva** points out: *'Mixing isn't the*

most important thing. It is equal amounts of selection and understanding of what makes people move and tick. You are a musical gauge or a musical interpreter.' We will cover more of this in chapter five as we work towards your first gig and pleasing the crowd.

And if you were thinking that once you've cracked mixing, the P word won't ever be mentioned again, well, you were wrong! ***'It's like a musical instrument. Like if I had a violin I wouldn't leave it in the box all week and then only play when I had to because it would sound awful. Whenever I go on my decks it's lethal: as soon as I put on my headphones that'll be it for two, three, four hours!'* – DJ Paulette.** You've been told.

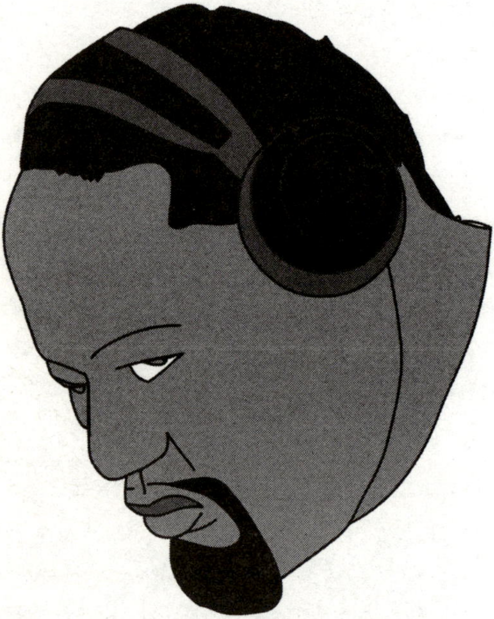

chapter four

your scratching arsenal

*❦ I heard Malcolm McLaren's **Buffalo Girls** and I talked to my art teacher, saying I liked the bit in the middle that went, wucka, wucka, wucka. And he said, "that's scratching, that is" ... ❦* – **prime cuts,** scratch perverts

history lesson two – scratching and battling

While DJs like Cool Herc were manipulating two records on turntables to extend the breakbeats, it was a thirteen-year-old kid called Theodore Livingstone (who called himself Grand Wizard Theodore) who invented the scratch in the late 70s'. He was playing loud music in his room one day and his mum came in to shout at him to turn it down. While she was standing in the doorway, nagging, he was moving the record back and forth under the needle to keep it in the same place and he heard the sound and liked what he heard – the scratch was born! It wasn't till later (1983) that it became mainstream, when Herbie Hancock released *Rockit* with DJ Grandmixer D.ST scratching on it. The song was a hit.

But how did battling come about? Well, DJs had always battled with their sound systems in New York. Cool Herc would stand with his enormous system against Grandmaster Flash and Afrika Bambaataa and blast them off the block with a wall of sound. That was how the battle culture began – seeing who was the loudest. Soon scratching battles were being set up as more and more scratches were invented and official competitions were organized to cater for this. The Dance Mix Club (DMC) held its first World Championship in 1987 and this is now the biggest DJ Battle arena in the world. DJs from all over come and pitch their skills against each other in team events and as solo performers. It wasn't until 1995 that the word 'turntablism' raised its head in the arena. DJ Babu from the Beat Junkies coined the phrase, describing turntablists as people who use two turntables to manipulate sound and create music.

Turntablists have all sorts of tricks up their sleeves: scratching, body tricks, back to backing and beat juggling. And we are going to check them out in this chapter, with help from a turntablist crew, the Plagia-wrists (DJs Olson, Precise and Proof) and Prime Cuts from the Scratch Perverts, two times DMC Team World Champ and two times ITF World Champ. But scratching is *much* harder than learning to beat match, so I suggest you try and figure that out first if you want to do both. You don't have to learn to beat match and mix before you can scratch, but most people do.

get started

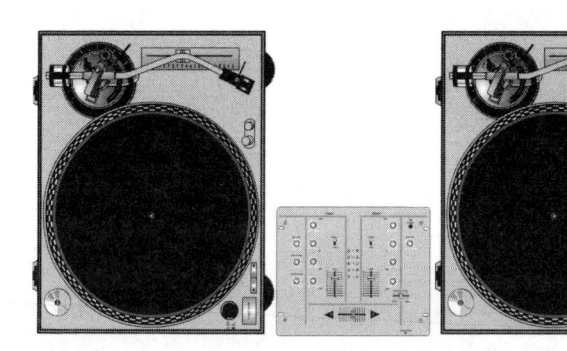

You need to set up your equipment to get the maximum out of it for scratching. First of all, if your turntable doesn't have a straight tone arm, you need to reset the cartridge (see chapter two) so that the needle is in line with the counterweight. The surface you are going to put the decks on needs to be really stable, so nothing jumps – so push a table right up against the wall to remedy any shakes and wedge paper under any wobbly table legs. **Prime Cuts** also stresses, if you are worried about jumpy needles: ***'Don't put pennies on the headshell – it's a death sentence for your records!'***

Next, place your decks lengthways on the table either side of the mixer. You want the tone arm to be at the top so that it is out of the way and you can't knock it when scratching. The mixer should be switched to the steep shelving curve on the curve adjust at the base of the mixer. Notice that when you slide the crossfader from the Off to the On position, instead of the cued-up tune coming in gradually, it cuts in almost immediately, giving you a good cut-in point for scratching.

Lots of people prefer to scratch hamster-style. This entails flipping the crossfader reverse switch on the base of the mixer so that you change round the channel output of the crossfader. Now you will have the crossfader slid over to the right on the mixer, but instead of deck B coming out of the speakers, it will be deck A and vice versa. **DJ Olson** from the Plagia-wrists explains: ***'If you don't have a mixer with a hamster switch, you can change the leads at the back of the mixer so that the crossfader is switched round.'*** You will have to try both methods and see what feels natural to you. It is hard to explain why some people find scratching hamster-style easier and the only way to see if it is for you is to try it!

You will definitely need to have that extra slippiness under your slipmat if you are scratching so, as before, get busy with the greaseproof paper or shiny plastic record inner sleeves.

waxing lyrical

Your choice of vinyl is really important for scratching – you need as many different sounds as possible. That's why battle weapon records are a good idea. They were created specifically for scratching by turntablists, and consist of lots of different samples: musical stabs (the beginning of a break), snare drums, kick drum, bass, vocal snippets (including aaaahs – literally the sound of someone singing just that!), long sounds and loops all laid down together on one twelve-inch. The Invisibl Skratch Piklz used one of their creations to win the first DMC World Team Championships. They have been making battle weapons since the early 90s.

Prime Cuts gives us advice on battle weapons: ***'The battle weapon that is best for someone who's just starting would be one of the few around at the moment with sounds cut into the vinyl so they hit at the same point. You will have a succession of the same sound pressed over a part of the vinyl, so that sound will always hit three o'clock – if the needle skips, you've always got the same sound. So you might be a bit heavy-handed while you're getting used to it, you don't have the frustration of, Argh – it's hopped again! There are a couple that are good for that: Seal Breaks, or Super Seal Breaks,***

one of Q-Bert's battle weapons. Most of the Dirt Star label battle weapons are good.'

Other classic battle weapons worth mentioning are Turntablist, *Super Duck Breaks* and Pancake Man, *Kleptomania*. You really need to go and have a listen and check out what sounds you want to scratch with. Also, why not raid your parents' record collection – you never know what prize guitar riffs are hiding in there! Charity shops are also good for picking up oddball scraps of vinyl.

make your mark

Now you have sorted out some scratch samples to work with – vocals and musical stabs are favourites – you'll want to be able to find them speedily each time, so to help you out, mark the records with a sticker. Use those stickers from cassette labels or buy some small rectangular ones from a stationer. Either slap the sticker on the label, pointing in the direction of the needle if the sample is nearer the middle of the record or on the edge if the sample is nearer the outside, again pointing towards the needle.

It isn't an exact pinpoint of which groove the sample starts in, but once you have found it in a matter of seconds rather than minutes, you can drag the record back to the original start point after the sample has been played.

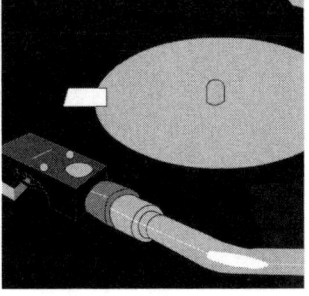

Another tip handed down by countless DJs – beware of wobbly records! This happens when the hole in the middle is too big for the spindle. All you do is ram a piece of tissue paper over the spindle and put the record on top. You might have to put on more than one piece, depending on the size of the hole.

get bizzy with it

Before you even think about scratching, **Prime Cuts** has these words to say: *'The hardest thing for anyone who has just started is to be able to manipulate the record back and forth without it drifting underneath your fingers. It's like learning the violin – it's a nightmare to try and hold the violin and get a note out of it. Scratching is a lot more instant than that ... there is a little bit of a learning curve in actually sussing how to move the record just simply backwards and forwards in a controlled manner.'* Got that? Switch the deck on and practise that backwards and forwards motion till you feel you are *au fait* with it. Another word – scratches are called different things to different people, so you will hear a forward called a cut and a stab, a chop – it doesn't matter, as long as you can do them!

baby scratch

The first scratch the Plagia-wrists recommend starting off with is the first one ever invented by Grand Wizard Theodore. Switch on the other deck and play a rhythm track. Keep the fader on what is known as the 'cut-in point' (from now on called the 'On' or 'Open' position) so you can hear both decks playing. You don't need to use the fader at all for this one, so just ignore it after that! Switch the other deck on too and find the sample you wish to scratch with – you will have marked up your record, so it will be easy to find! Line the beginning of the sample up with the needle and then start moving the vinyl forwards to the end of the sample and then backwards to the beginning in time with the beat from the other deck. You must drag the record back to the original start point each time before moving it forwards again, which is what the sticker is for. And that's the baby scratch!

the chop/stab

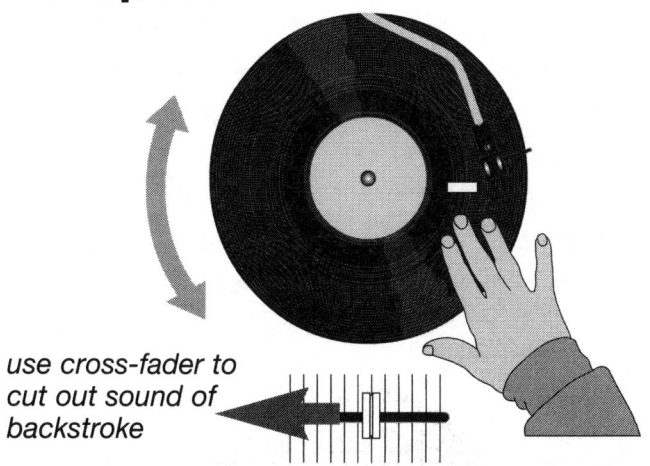

use cross-fader to cut out sound of backstroke

You really need a mixer with a sharp cut-in here in order to scratch properly, so make sure the curve adjust is switched to the short mix. And if you want to scratch hamster-style (reverse), which a lot of DJs do rather than having the crossfader in the normal position, then flip the reverse switch. The Plagia-wrists scratch in hamster all the time. **Precise** says: *'I think it's easier to get your head round hamster-style than normal. The important thing here is to make it easy for yourself.'* DJ Olson suggests trying both ways to see what you personally feel comfortable with.

Start with the fader open (which could be to the left or the right, depending on whether you are hamster or not) and the needle at the beginning of the sample. The hand movement you are going to use is the same as the baby scratch, but the difference is, you are going to cut out the sound of the backstroke using the crossfader. Move the vinyl forwards in time with the other record's beat, and as you come to the end of the forward stroke, close the fader, cutting off the reverse motion as you bring the record back to the beginning of the sample to start again. You won't hear the reverse scratch because the fader is closed. When you are back to where the sticker is indicating the start of the sample, open the fader and repeat. The sound you've made should be a short sudden scratch.

You can do this in reverse as well. Start with the needle at the end of the sample and the fader 'On' so that you can hear both decks. Drag the sample back to the beginning in time with the beat from the other deck. When you reach the sticker marking the beginning of the sample, close the fader to shut the sound off and scratch or let the vinyl fly forwards to the end of the sample to start again. Done!

important tip!

With these two scratches and the baby scratch, you already have enough moves to put together a small routine. Practise moving between all three in time to the beat on the other deck. Remember too – you have to put some thought behind what you are doing. The scratches have to make musical sense with the other piece of music that is playing over the speakers. Listen to other scratch DJs and hip-hop records with scratching on them – the scratching is part of the tune as well as being layered over the top of it – they work together to create a new sound.

the transformer

'Transforming is one of the most important things you should be able to do' – **DJ Precise**. Start with the crossfader in the closed position and the needle at the beginning of your chosen sample and move the vinyl forwards and backwards under the needle. The fader should then be used to repeatedly cut the sound in and straight back out again to create a stutter effect in time with the music on the other deck. At the end of the scratch the crossfader should be in the 'Off' position. DJ Proof reminds us that if we do the transformer at different speeds, both scratching and the clicking fader have to be speeded up in tandem.

the forward

This is almost the same as the chop/stab. Start with the fader open and instead of scratching the vinyl forward from the beginning of the sample, you let it play to the end of the sample at normal speed. Once the sample has played, you cut off the sound by closing the fader, bringing the sample silently back to the beginning, ready to play again. This scratch works really well with a vocal snippet, especially an 'aaaah'!

tears

For this scratch, you want the fader in the open position and the needle at the start of your sample. The fader doesn't come into play. Now, you are going to move the vinyl forwards and backwards in time to the other beat like a baby scratch. BUT, instead of one movement forwards, you are going to play the sample in two segments by putting a sort of 'jolt' in the middle, in time with the music. When you reach the end of the sample, drag the record back under the needle to the start and do it again.

You can do a tear in reverse. Start at the beginning

of the sample and move the record forwards under the needle and as you drag it back to the start where the sticker is, do so in two segments, with a 'jolt' in the middle. You can do a tear on the forward and backstroke, and as you get hotter and hotter at scratching, you can do multiple tears with more than one jolt on the forward or backward motion or both! This scratch is really versatile and a good one to start off with, as you can really play around with it to create different rhythms. As you add more 'jolts' it is really hard to keep in time with the other piece of music at first, but practice will help you there!

the chirp

Now we are getting into the realms of patting your head while rubbing your tummy! This requires a lot more hand coordination than the other scratches. With the chirp, you are using the crossfader to cut off the beginning and end of the sample, so all you will hear is the middle part, giving the scratch its characteristic 'chirping' sound.

Start with the fader open and the needle at the beginning of your sample. Move the vinyl forwards in time with the beat and, towards the end of the sample, close the fader to fade out the end of the sample. Now open up the fader while dragging back the vinyl to the start of the sample but, as you approach the start, you have to close the fader again to cut off the sound. Understand? No? Maybe the diagram over the page will help.

This move is very hard to explain on paper and the only way you will get it is to stop reading and go and try it immediately, now – go on! A reprise: forward stroke – fader on, end sample – fader off. Backstroke – fader on, back at beginning – fader off. Forward stroke – fader on, end of sample – fader off. Backstroke fader on, back to beginning – fader off, and so on and so on, etc., etc., amen … If you move the record twice as fast in time with the beat, the crossfader has to follow just as fast like a lost puppy! My head is spinning.

the flare

Funnily enough, this was invented by DJ Flare, an honorary member of the Invisibl Skratch Piklz in the late 80s. The flare uses the crossfader to cut out the middle of the sample, just catching the beginning and the end. As **DJ Precise** says: *'Flares are wicked because it sounds like you are doing it twice as fast when you aren't!'*

'Yeah, a chirp sounds like: chig-chig,

chig-chig, whereas a flare sounds like: dibbet, dibbet, dibbet – it doubles it with only one click!' – **DJ Olson**

To find out how this sounds, start with the fader in the Open position and the needle on the start of the sample. Move the record forwards in time with the beat and quickly click the fader off and then on again, to cut out the middle of the sample. As you drag the record back, do the same: clicking the fader off then on, to cut out the middle of the sample on the reverse. You have to get the clicks in the same spot of the sample during the backstroke as you do on the forward stroke (now they tell us!)

use crossfader to cut out middle of sample as record is pushed forward

use crossfader to cut out middle of sample as record is pulled back

You can add more clicks to the flare – a two-click flare is called an orbit and you have to fit in two clicks of a 'closed–open, closed–open' crossfader before you reach the end of the sample. Would you believe it – people do a three-click flare? You'd better practise before you even think about it. As with all the other scratches, you can mix and match and do a one-click flare on the forward stroke and two-clicks on the reverse – whatever, the world's your oyster, or maybe it's a crab …

the crab

How nimble are your fingers? Loose enough to manage the crab? You do need a decent crossfader to do this as well as well-oiled fingers. To start with we are going to describe this in the hamster position (known as hamster crab) as opposed to normal crab. The fader should be in the Open position with your thumb over the Closed position and your four fingers placed vertically on the other side of the fader.

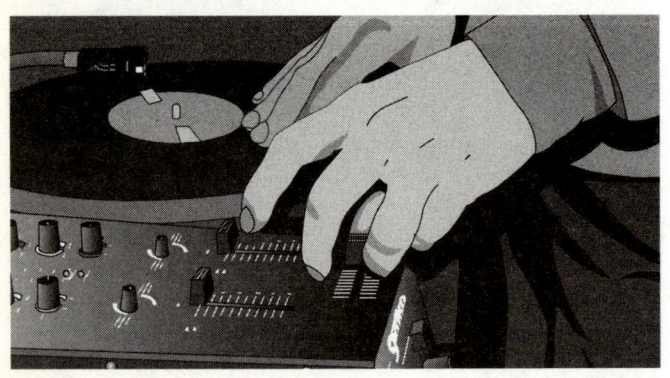

Try doing the crab on its own without the decks, just to get used to the movement. So starting with your little finger first, flick the fader closed towards the thumb, which returns it to the Open position, acting like a buffer. Follow this with your ring finger, then middle and finally index finger, making a rhythmical flicking motion like the movements of a crab's legs! When you have got the hang of it, try it with both decks working, and move the vinyl backwards and forwards so you can hear the crab cutting the sound out then in and out and in, etc. ... You can do the crab in the normal position, but this time you would be opening the fader with the crab movement, not shutting it.

back to backing and beat juggling

DJ Precise takes us through the original manipulation of breaks, with which Cool Herc started off in the Bronx – back to backing. You need two copies of the same record (not vital, they can be records with similar drum breaks) and you should mark them up in the same place with a sticker where the decent drum break is. You will want to have the mixer on normal and not reverse for this or you could end up getting confused!

Slide the fader over to the deck that you are going to release the first break from, let's say record A. You've released record A and it is playing over the speakers. As the drum break comes to an end, slide the fader across to record B and release that one, extending the break. Meanwhile, you will have rewound record A back to the starting point of the break marked by the sticker, and when record B's break starts to finish, you are ready to slide the fader across and start again. This is not as easy as it sounds and you should practise it till you can do it in your sleep.

When you start adding extra drums, you are entering into the realms of beat juggling. This is much harder than back to backing as you have to actually make the patterns you are creating make musical sense, rather than sound like a barrage of machine-gun fire. Start off by releasing record B too early and at different points in the break while record A is still playing to create a different sound altogether. Experiment and see what you can come up with. Beat juggling when done really well sounds amazing and quite groovy – depending on what sort of drum breaks on vinyl you have to work with in the first place.

These are by no means all the scratches there are in the world, but they are the only ones you need to know right now. As you improve, you can try the more difficult ones and string together the ones you do know into intricate patterns. But, as **DJ Olson** says, *'**Don't run before you can walk. You should learn the foundations before you start doing things like the crab. You should be able to do the basics in a very relaxed manner without even thinking about it. Like you are playing a musical instrument, not like you are a robot!**'* So keep practising those tears, baby scratches, forwards and chops before you let yourself loose on anything else!

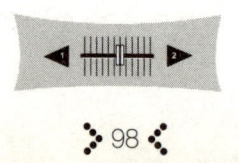

hip-hop clubbing

So, with all these skills, would you use them in a club environment or are they all strictly battling arsenal? I asked **Prime Cuts** how he used them …

'When we play drum'n'bass, you won't see us scratching or working the records that heavy. But we will use EQ trickery in a different way to most people … We try to keep our main focus on the dance floor because that's what it's about in a club. It's not about you and how good you are at scratching; it's about maximum effect for the dance floor. Me, Tony (Vegas) and Neil (Plus One), we break things down and we go crazy for about twenty seconds and everyone goes "Aaaawwwww!" And then we hit them with a really good record and you've kind of elevated the atmosphere and you keep trying to built it and build it …'

Wise words indeed – less is more and a good way to tease a crowd, but what about a battle? How do you work that out? The Plagia-wrists face a battle with four to six decks: *'You can work it a little bit like a band, with someone cutting up drums. You cut the kick drum and the snare together and create a rhythm like that'* – **DJ Precise**

prepare for battle

When you start to get really good at scratching, you might think about entering a battle, but what is the easiest way to prepare? Routines are normally about six to seven minutes long and DJs can get through as many as thirty records, so it obviously has to be planned right down to the last second. **Prime Cuts** was on tour when he decided to defend his 1999 ITF World Champion title in 2000. *'I did it on paper. In a battle you've got a time-constraint and you've really got to make every second count. And you've got to make it musical, have it build, have it end on a crazy ending, so that's what's left in people's minds when you walk away from it.*

'The composing on paper thing really works because it allows you to step away from it, whereas if you are on the turntables, you are in it. I came up with the different sections alongside a timeline,

thinking this is the first fifteen seconds, this is the middle thirty seconds – trying to make everything fit into that routine. Of course, you perform it about a hundred times with a stopwatch before you do it onstage – shaving here and there or adding things in. It's always good to have it a bit under so you can't go over.'

You can't get nervous in a battle – there's nothing worse than trembling fingers for scratching, but Prime Cuts has seen a lot of top names get the shakes. Keep that in mind if you ever get a case of jelly fingers!

dissing

This is an important part of battling and it's all in good humour. Everyone does it – it means poking fun or gently bad-mouthing your opponents as part of the routine. **Prime Cuts** relays one of his disses at the ITF World Finals 2000: *'I was against two people, one guy from Scotland and one from New York City. The guy from Scotland was virtually unknown, so I decided not to diss him, because I knew that would be a diss in itself! I went for the other guy because I knew he was good. He was a well-proportioned guy; he was large all over! I just went through some records – it's* *an easy target, and you can get some funny disses on hip-hop records – and found an old Roxanne Chante record. I think she says: "You better hurry and hop on a diet plan, and keep the pork chops out the frying pan!" So I did the whole routine and ended on that. The crowd wet themselves laughing!'* Of course, he regained the title! Now go and see how many disses you can dig out on records at home …

oops, I did it again…

Invariably things are going to go wrong – even to experienced DJs. The Scratch Perverts lost their World DMC title in 2000 because they made a few mistakes and never fully recovered the routine. Prime Cuts admits they over-complicated the routine, making it hard to pull off, so from that snippet of info you should remember to keep it simple and leave out anything you are not one hundred per cent capable of. But what happens if you do make a mistake?

How do you get out of that hole? *'I think the most important thing is to totally make sure you can do it with your eyes shut. If something goes wrong, just smile about it; most people won't know anything's gone wrong apart from you … I've judged quite a*

few competitions and I've seen people mess it up, and I'll mark someone favourably if they style it and kind of cover it. If someone grimaces and shakes their head, you've just defeated yourself there and then. You need to be like, I'm so good, I made the mistake look good!' – **Prime Cuts**

On that note, I think it's time for you to practise what you've gathered from this chapter. All scratches are a variation on a theme, so it isn't really the scratches that make a turntablist, it's the way they put together those scratches in musical sequences that makes them stand out from the crowd. So, if you think you've just come up with the new double-ended-jam-sandwich-juggle scratch then, in all honesty, you probably haven't because it's really called the peanut-butter-drill-forward-stab somewhere else. All you can do for now, till you are elevated to the standard of genius, like Q-Bert and his Invisibl Skratch Piklz, is do your best and make sure you do the jam-sandwich-juggle scratch better than anyone else – ever.

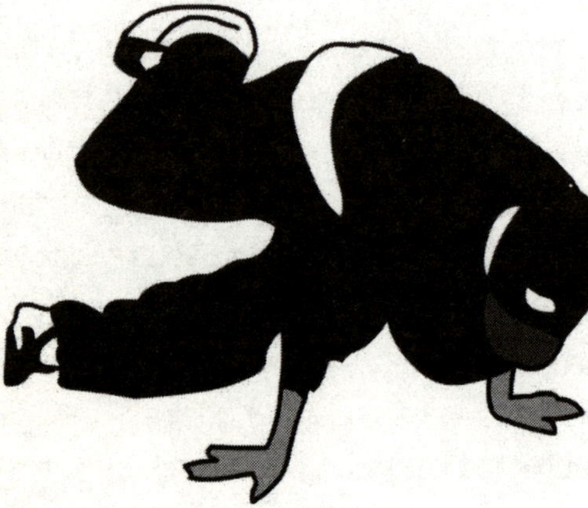

chapter five

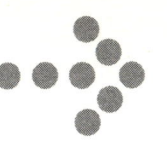

let's get this party started

"You've got to be strong enough to stand the knock-backs and take it again and again" – graham gold

By now you will have been surgically attached to your decks for months and your friends will have given up trying to coax you out from your pit. Hopefully you'll really feel like you've made progress and your mixing is getting somewhere, but what now? Where do you go from here, if indeed you do want to take your sound out of the bedroom and unleash it on to an unsuspecting world? If you *have* decided you want to share your love of music with the masses, or just your friends, then you might want to check out these ideas …

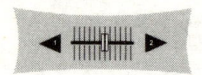

you gotta be starting something

'What kids have to do is try and create their own thing. That's what the UK garage lot did – they weren't getting a look in anywhere. They couldn't break into the house scene, so they started their own nights … They created their own market' – **St.John de Zilva.** Hosting your own parties is a guaranteed way of getting on the decks and building a name, no matter how small you start …

Until you are at an age where you can actually start up your own night as DJ/promoter, why not ask the parents if you can have a party at home to test your talent on a group of mates? At least if you make any clangers, there isn't going to be anyone there to pull you off the decks. **'The first time we played it was to twenty people in someone's front room. It was great fun and you are allowed to be not so confident and a bit rubbish because it isn't a club and no one is losing any money'** – DJ/producer **Bob Bhamra**

But don't forget to tell your neighbours in advance

that you're having a party – and please don't vibrate their pictures off the walls with your thumping bass.

If you want to progress from the living room, but are still not the legal age for organizing a gig in a local bar/pub, then take a leaf out of **DJ Paulette**'s book: *'Build up your own following. Start a night at a youth club between twelve and eighteen, and by the time you are old enough to go to clubs, then you've got a crowd to start a club with, so it's not coming from nowhere.'* Just enquire at the local youth club/community centre; see what channels you have to go through to get it approved, if you need to hire any equipment, etc. Then start the ball rolling with the publicity wagon: you can make posters, tell all your friends, leave flyers anywhere that will let you, perhaps at school, and at the venue itself. A following is what it's all about: *'You're only ever going to be a superstar DJ if you have a following … And a following has gotta start somewhere, so what better place than you getting all your friends and their friends coming down to see you DJ?'* – **Ali B**, Capital Radio

School is also a great place to try out your talents – everyone loves a school party and assembly halls are perfect. Ask a teacher/grovel/offer to clean toilets just so you can hold a school party for the whole year/school. Do it for charity so that they can't refuse!

Checking out real DJs and clubs needn't be off limits any more. Every half term, and during the school holidays, there are under-eighteen club nights. More and more towns are doing them, and they are held in proper clubs throughout the country. Leisure centres also hold them at weekends. Check the papers for details or listing magazines like *Time Out* or similar ones for your area. Go along and see how it is done properly – steal ideas for your own nights! Also, why not try and get a gig at one of these nights? Send in a mix tape (more about these later on) to the promoter – they usually have their name on the flyer or on the advert in the paper, with a contact number. You have nothing to lose!

When you get older and if you are going for a bar, you will have to have the gift of the gab and convince the owner that you can make them money by bringing in a big crowd. That's how Ali B started off Blue Print, in a small bar on a Sunday, and it really worked, leading on to bigger and better things. Now he has his own show on Capital Radio and is a Fabric regular. Again, check out the place's equipment. Their mixer might be really ancient and in need of replacement, so take along your own. And carts too – they will have been hanging around for years probably if this venue doesn't do regular nights – so take a spare set in case they pack up (it has happened to me). Also, if you are in a bar, you have to be prepared to be wallpaper music for a lot of the night, as people will be chatting – it isn't like a club.

Flyers are easy to make; get on a computer and get busy with some glue and scissors and photocopy a bold design, just detailing the type of music (the most important ingredient) and not bigging yourself up, people aren't that interested – honest – not yet anyway! Not until you build up a following … **Fiona Wraith**, whose club, the Kindergarten, is a favourite of Danny Rampling, started off doing everything: *'For the first year we worked really hard on promotion. We handed out all the flyers ourselves, designed everything to do with the club, dressed the club before the night, did themed nights. Word of mouth got round and it got really popular.'* Make that effort – you want to create the right sort of vibe and transform that youth club/school disco into a buzzing danceatoria.

If there is more than one of you DJing, you need to work out an order and build the night up from warm-up set of head-shaking, feet-tapping beats through to banging, full-on dancing. There is no point playing eye-popping techno when three people are standing around waiting for everyone to arrive. Allocate time slots to DJs, or you could have a case of 'Just one more tune, mate, honest, then I'll get off.' You will be surprised how egos can expand after a smidgen of adulation behind the decks.

As you build up that following and people ask you to DJ at places, parties – do it. *'For a good five or six years I would DJ anywhere. I've dragged my decks out to dodgy parties, just to play. Put yourself round as much as possible. Once you've learned all that grass-roots stuff and you can make a bunch of forty-*

year-olds in a pub dance, you can do anything!' – **St.John de Zilva**. Never turn a gig down – you never know what it might lead on to …

other ways to get ahead …

If you are really serious about what you are doing and know you want to DJ for your career, you can go to DJ schools and learn the trade from professionals. St.John de Zilva runs free DJ Workshops for eleven- to sixteen-year-olds in south London and takes the workshops out to youth clubs and art centres around the country.

You don't have to have any experience at all, as all courses start with the basics, from Absolute Beginners, followed by Beginners and then Intermediate. If you don't have decks and there is no way you can afford them, a course like this is ideal.

St.John also runs a year-long BTEC course at Lewisham College, south London – a dance music and DJ workshop course, based on the DJ Workshops. At the end of it you will get a BTEC National Diploma for Performing Arts. *'The courses involve everything from basic mixing to putting on your own club night. The BTEC unit will also cover the technical side of things: how to get started, basic mixes, mixes right into things like fazing, echo, delay, dubbing up on beats using two copies of the same record. I only take it up to Intermediate stage because stylistically it's up to them how they want to develop.'*

Students go on to play in a club environment at the end of the courses. Many of St.John's students have gone on to work in pirate radio, make their own music, start their own labels and promote their own nights. **'I think you need those skills to make it. The more skills and perseverance you have means you'll just have an independent hand on things.'** Check out the web site www.djworkshop.co.uk for more information on mixing and scratching courses.

There are other courses available around the country, but you have to pay for a lot of them. Do ask your local authority about free courses, as some councils run them too. DJ courses are springing up everywhere now, and some entrepreneurs are seeing it as a way to make a lot of money, so beware – investigate anything thoroughly before you hand over any money. It can cost up to £600 for a six-week course. Check out this web site – it gives independent advice on courses you can pay for, as well as other music-industry advice: www.likemusic.com. Hit the Music Careers icon to download course info.

pirate radio

Lots of today's big name DJs started off on pirate radio: Danny Rampling, Norman Jay, Judge Jules and, more recently, UK garage stars, Genius Cru, heralding from Flex FM. Listen in to ones in your area and hear how much more underground the tunes are than on Radio One and commercial stations. A lot of the DJs will have made the records themselves and this is the only way to get any air play – it is also another avenue for getting noticed and being unique. If you want to find out which stations you can tune into, log on to www.pirateradiouk.com for a complete list of all the best UK stations and the history of pirate radio – fascinating stuff! (By the way, you should know that pirate radio stations are illegal. They operate on unlicensed frequencies and can be raided, shut down and those involved prosecuted by the DTI's Radio Communications Agency (www.gov.uk))

DJ Leon plays on Flex FM and says pirates are notoriously difficult to get on, and in most cases you have to pay *them* for a slot! You also have to know someone at the station to get your foot in the door. But **St.John de Zilva** points out: **'Inevitably with pirates, they are on late at night. You have to be willing to do the graveyard shift – from three to six in the morning. I know a few of my students, through DJ Workshop, have managed to get sets on pirates ... Once you have that graveyard slot, you're in there, you can move around. It's just a very good grass-roots way of establishing yourself; getting people to know you.'** St.John started on pirate Girls FM after a tape he sent in for a competition won him a slot: **'We had stupid moments. The electricity went off – the lights went off, the decks were still on – I had to mix in total darkness for two hours! I couldn't see the**

records. It was a really good experience, but I'm not advocating that kids go on pirate stations!' Not a place for anyone under eighteen or still at school, but still good to listen to and catch remixes of tunes and original music that you won't hear anywhere else. You could be listening to the stars of the future!

Internet radio stations are also a good way of getting yourself noticed and maybe kick-starting a career as a DJ. Look on the Net for dance music stations and see if you can find a source to send a tape to. Listen to some of the more established ones, and watch out for new ones popping up weekly:
www.ministryofsound.com, www.groovetech.com, www.gaialive.co.uk, www.space.fm.co.uk.

mix tapes – your first impression

Ahhh, there is an art to making a good mix tape/CD. They are essential for self-promotion and you will need to send one off to club promoters (if you are trying for an under-eighteen club gig) and your youth club, so they know you can DJ before you try to get a night going. Do they work though? Mixed feelings on the matter …

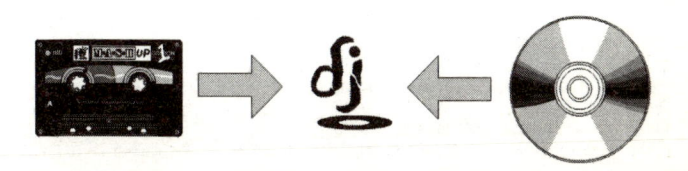

how do you choose the tunes?

'I take it from a typical set I play. It is quite difficult to do a tape. Another easy way is to do three tapes. A warm up, a middle set and a peak set, and that way you can pick from what you play. However, promoters prefer CDs ...' – **Wes**, Plastic Fantastic Records, regular DJ at The Cross, London.

'If I hear a mix tape that just goes hit, hit, hit, I just throw it out the car! I look for something that's different, excites me – the way they mix. But I don't do it any more ...' – **Graham Gold**, Kiss FM and resident at Peach. Be original! A load of anthems isn't going to get you a gig, unless you cut them up in an amazing fashion.

should you make an effort with cover design?

'If you put it in a big box with a bow on it, that would probably put us off, more likely! If people send an email or make a phone call to let us know it is coming, when it does arrive, you tend to put the two together and it stands out that way' – **Jason Ellis** at Positiva talking about artist CDs – but the same applies to mix tapes.

Keep it simple: *'If you get on a flyer, grab a handful and send it out with the CD. Don't be ashamed of getting together a CV of what you've done and what your interests are'* – **Fiona Wraith**, Kindergarten Klub

what if you never get the call?

'Keep persisting! You need to practise and make CDs/tapes. There's no point sending out a tape you made back in March in July because you will have improved by then. Just keep sending new CDs' – **Fiona Wraith**

some djs/promoters don't trust mix tapes...

'I did listen to tapes for putting people into Peach and there were a couple who really stood out. You could tell they'd thought about what set they were playing. And then we did put on a few of these young fellas and they just went hit, hit, hit. And I was thinking, I didn't book you for that – that wasn't on your tape!' – **Graham Gold**. You need to deliver the goods and stay true to what the promoter has booked you for (i.e. the type of music on your tape) or you won't get asked back again.

so, will mix tapes get you work, even if you are a young 'un?

'If we think someone is good, no matter what age, we will give them a chance. They can send in CDs and we would try them out in the first hour when it's quiet. If they are any good we will invite them back. It's always in your interest as a club promoter to try new people. You can become complacent about your music and if you've got someone who isn't always

***one hundred per cent, it shows. You need to keep it fresh. You need commitment to finding new music!'* – Fiona Wraith**.

Really, it just depends on the club. Some clubs won't give anyone a chance and stick with old faithfuls, whereas smaller clubs will give mix tapes a chance. As Fiona mentioned, keep plugging away if you are that keen for a club slot.

tip!

Send mix tapes into dance-music magazines – they always run competitions for best mix tape. Most famously, Yousef won Bedroom Bedlam from *Muzik Magazine,* which lead to his big break and a residency at Cream in Liverpool. Enter competitions too – anything to get your name seen.

age is only a number

Don't be put off if people don't take you seriously, as there are other kids out there, making names for themselves: PJ the DJ and DJ Kingy, for example. Hard house king Fergie started out aged twelve in Ireland, playing gigs standing on top of a milk crate to reach the decks! If you are talented, under-eighteen promoters would be stupid not to give you a warm-up slot – imagine the crowd seeing someone their age up there behind the decks, how cool is that?! You have got age on your side and you should remember that. It is an ace up your sleeve, as the younger you are the more of a novelty you are. That is what everyone is looking for these days, the Next Big Thing – and it could be you! Bingo! **'Start young; learn as much as you can while you're young. Get your foot in the door while you're fresh and exciting, while you're new talent'** – **Lisa Loud**. You heard the lady! Just make sure your parents don't mind you earning more money than them.

As if ….

image is everything!

Yawn – yes, can't get away without mentioning this. It used to be that most male DJs could stand behind a pair of decks in a string vest with a big fat beer gut hanging out, sweating like a hot-house flower – not that they did, but you got the impression it wouldn't have mattered if they had. As long as they were great at what they did – and quite right too. BUT, this has never been the case for women DJs and it is changing more and more for the guys. Can you imagine Lisa Lashes without her make-up or Lottie without her trademark fringe swinging in her eyes and her cool trainers? Where would Judge Jules be without his mad shirts and funky little specs or Roger Sanchez without his little hat and neatly trimmed goatee? And can you imagine Run DMC without any phat trainers? No way, man! Maybe it's time to ditch those hole-in-the-knee jeans and get something a bit more stylish …

what's in a name?

A lot it seems, especially in the turntablist world. Not all DJs have special names, but those who do, you tend to remember: Judge Jules, the Dreem Teem, the Chemical Brothers (used to be called the Dust Brothers), Fat Boy Slim (previous name Pizza Man!), EZ, Basement Jaxx, Tall Paul and the Stanton Warriors (they got their name from a manhole cover – there is inspiration everywhere!)

But it is in the turntablist world that it matters the most. All crews have cool names and every DJ within the crew has a name too. There is Q-Bert and his Invisibl Skratch Piklz, The Scratch Perverts – Prime Cuts, Tony Vegas and Plus One, DJ Babu from the Beat Junkies, DJ Cash Money, DJ Food, DJ Vadim, A-Trak, etc. So, get your thinking cap on and come up with an original name that will set you apart from everyone else – something that says a bit about you or your taste in music.

it's a girl thing

This whole image thing is especially important for

women. Not only do they have to look good, but they have to be brilliant too. Check out what some top female DJs have to say about it all:

🔘 *'Think of a good girlie DJ name. This is SO important to promoters. Get a DJ name that is clear to everyone you are a woman'* – **Miss Behavin'**

🔘 *'I think increasingly as the business grows and grows ... you have to have an image. You've got to look like something; you've got to portray a reflection of what you are about in your music and your style as a faceless commodity'* – **Lisa Loud**

🔘 Some people won't take you seriously: *'When I first started DJing, a lot of people in the industry tried to put me down because I was female, but that just made me more determined to succeed. So, thanks to the guy I bought my first decks from who told me: "The only type of mixing you'll be good for, darling, is cake mixing!!!" Comments like that just used to make me think, Right, I'll show 'em!'* – **Miss Behavin'**

🔘 **DJ Paulette** finds it still happens even when you are successful: *'I am funny about people driving me to gigs and carrying my record box. As soon as a bloke walks in with your record box, they (the crowd) think he's the DJ and you're just some daft bird. And then*

you put the headphones on and they have a heart attack!'

People will stare and wait for you to mess up, it happens all the time, but just ignore them, though it is hard when they are ten men deep! You can get the bouncers to move them for you – DJ Paulette has done in the past. It is very off-putting.

Do women DJs have to work harder to get recognized though? DJ Paulette thinks it is just the same in any industry, and for life in general. If you want something, you need to go for it and work hard, no matter if you are male or female.

Lisa Loud has more specific advice: ***'Craft your style and have an idea where you are going musically, because you won't be taken seriously otherwise (that goes for men and women, but particularly women); craft your technique ... You've kind of put yourself in the boys' club because you're being a bit nerdy, a bit technical, that might sound ridiculous, but that's what the music press want if they're going to cover you. They want you to be serious about your music. And being technical and knowing your style and knowing your music is going to get you that coverage.'***

UK garage DJ **Femme Fatal** agrees: ***'Don't think being female will get you noticed. Go to places industry people hang out and meet the people and go again and again!***

Make the most of every opportunity that comes your way.' If you're serious about DJing, take note!

If you have sorted out a night, whether you are doing your own or have finally managed to get a gig at that under-eighteen club, what do you do? It's no longer your four mates in the bedroom – it is a room/club full of people waiting for you to show them a good time. Don't fall to pieces and sob under the decks, you need to move swiftly to chapter six, where our panel of experts can guide you through that first gig so it runs as smoothly as a banana in a blender …

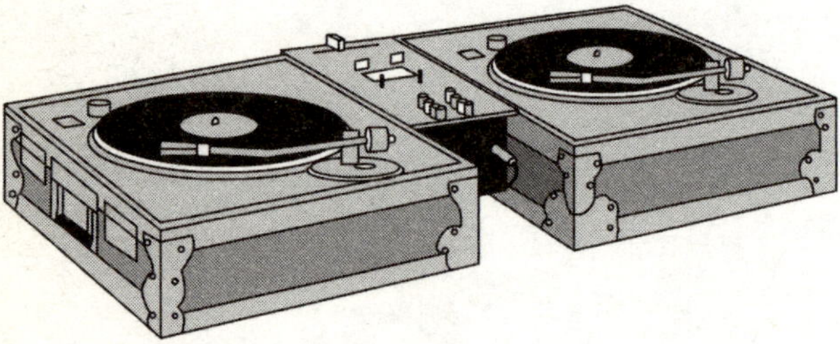

chapter six

it's show time

I've had loads of bad nights. Fights, not being paid, rows with bouncers, people spilling drinks over my records ... you name it! – judge jules

first-night nerves

Every single DJ has had to do the first gig of their life and been as terrified as a turkey at Christmas ... probably. You are not the first and you won't be the last.

'I'd been practising in my bedroom for about two years and never thought I'd have the guts to become a DJ – until a mate of mine was DJing to three thousand people at a Mix Mag party and he left mid-set to go to the loo and forced me to put some tunes on while he was gone! I had no time to be nervous ... which was excellent!' – Miss

Behavin' thrown to the lions and loving it.

'I can't remember my first DJ set, but one early one that stands out is a night when I went to Jacqueline's in London's West End, and was suddenly asked to take over the DJ set using someone else's records, as they had just been fired ... I do remember being a little nervous that time!' – **Karl 'Tuff Enuff' Brown** proving even big boys can get a bit wobbly sometimes.

Wes from Plastic Fantastic Records had his first gig *as a warm-up at the Ministry of Sound: 'I was very nervous. I don't think I realized what I was doing. I was like – I am playing the Ministry of Sound, God! I didn't do what I wanted to do and I made a right cock-up. I was cross with myself.'*

Femme Fatal has advice on nerves: *'If it's a big gig I will go to the Ladies and give myself two minutes' space to empty my head and get in the zone.'* Boys, don't be literal – if you go to the Ladies, chances are you won't get to play the gig, you will be on your ear outside ...

get ready for anything

The Boy Scouts motto is 'Be prepared'. Take this on board; write it on the inside of your record box if necessary to keep it in your head.

🔘 Always get to the gig in loads of time so you can chill for a while. What is the point of collapsing in a sweaty heap after legging it there because you were late and got lost? You have a night of work ahead of you – be cool.

'Sort out your box properly. I have the records in sections – so I have instrumentals and vocals, DJ tools, a cappellas, edits and a very small section which is if you can't get them to dance, play this!' – **St.John de Zilva**, DJ Workshop

⚫ Check out the mixer with the previous DJ or sound engineer so you know where the headphone and monitor volumes are – they are not broken, you just can't figure them out in your cold sweat! Most mixers are the same really, some just have more flashing lights and tend to look like flight decks – don't panic, you will be able to use it!

⚫ Find out as much as you can about the gig and who else is playing. You might even put together some mixes at home beforehand. **'I find out what time I'm playing, who's on before me, who's on after me, because I think that's important, and if I know Jules is on before me, he's gonna play this, this and this, so I work it out at home. Not record for record, but just if I know whom I'm following then I know where I have to start. So I'll have the first four definitely worked out and then just work it out as I go along'** – **Graham Gold**, Kiss FM. In general, nobody works out a whole set at home because you have to tailor it to the crowd.

let me entertain you

Now, you may think that all the skills you need to make it as a DJ you can learn in your bedroom at home, practising on the decks. Yes, you can hone your mixing/scratching skills till you are blue in the face, but if you can't read a crowd you might as well get your coat …

What you also have to remember when you are starting out is that you may well have to compromise your sound slightly if you want to get a gig in the first place. Not everyone shares your passion for rib-rattling jungle: **'A lot of the youngsters don't understand and get cross. I get a lot of young DJs playing house, techno, trance, garage or whatever and they are very set on it. They've got to learn to be a bit more flexible or you won't get the experience you need unless you get very lucky. There are two routes there – you can either be frustrated in your bedroom and do no gigs, or decide to do local pubs and clubs. There is a way of doing it, integrating your own music. It's good to learn your trade and learn how your records can affect people's moods'** – St.John de Zilva

What sort of music you play really depends on what slot you have: warm-up, middle or peak time. It will be warm up if it is your first club gig, but if it is your own night in a youth club/party, you might do the whole night, in which case you have to have every type of record going! Unless, of course, you have mates helping you out.

'In a warm-up set never play anthems, just play nice beats and grooves, percussion. If I am playing a warm-up set at The Cross, I play funky, tribal-driven stuff, some vocals

now and then. The sort of way to describe it is you are standing at the bar having a drink and can get involved in the music, but you don't have to if you don't want to. If you want to go over and dance, you can because it's got that edge to it' – **Wes** from Plastic Fantastic Records

DJing in slots is rather like being in a relay, passing the baton on to the next member of the team. *'Don't give everything away at the start of the night so you've burnt your punters out. Be clever; build it up so when the superstar DJ goes on, not only are they going to be content, but happy that they can carry the night on and the punters are content because they've got a full night of really great music and they really respect you'* – **Lisa Loud**

'Every club set-up is different. Sometimes the decks are quite far away from the crowd, which is bad. You need to know what's going on down there – is it too loud, not loud enough? If I'm playing somewhere where I don't know the sound, I'll put two records on and then go for a little wander ... See what people are into – are they into it? People don't do that enough' – **Ali B**. You need to keep eye contact with the crowd if you can. If the dance floor is filling up, emptying – you need to know. What you have to remember is that you

are there for *them*, not you, and that means you listen to them, look at what is getting them going. **'I always picture myself as one of the clubbers and appreciate how the set sounds from their perspective. If you use too many mix tricks it can detract from the entertainment, so you have to get the balance right'** – **Karl 'Tuff Enuff' Brown**

If you play a load of obscure pressings that no one has ever heard, but you think are really amazing and are sure everyone will go mental for, what happens in most cases is people will lose interest and wander off. Only when you have the crowd in the palm of your hand can you unleash stuff like that – you are building up their trust. **DJ Paulette** suggests, **'Play one they don't know, one they do, one they don't know, one they do, etc. You're educating. There's got to be something there for everyone.'**

If the crowd aren't responding to your music at all, don't be afraid to try some big tunes – don't be too snobby about it, those tunes are big for a reason! **'You should have at least ten to fifteen safety nets in your box – your get-out-of-jail cards. If all else fails, these are your little gems and can bring people back to you. Sometimes you can do it too with being technically able. You can cut it up, do a bit of scratching, drop things in, drop things out. Because it's exciting, that might bring people to you'** – **Lisa Loud**

◗ You also want to get noticed, not be just another DJ warming up for someone else. ***'Taking a risk will make you stand out – play something no one expects. They might laugh, think it's silly, or whatever, but everyone will remember that night!'*** – DJ/producer **Bob Bhamra**

◗ Big name DJs also play remixes of tunes that they have done on CDs or acetate and no one else will have them. As you get more and more experienced, you will find that this is the way to make your sets original. Most DJs nowadays are producers too and it is almost necessary to make music and get into producing to further your career. Just concentrate on doing your first gig though for now!

◗ As you do more gigs, you will start to notice that crowd connection and reading the dance floor will become second nature. ***'I know it sounds poncy, but when you do feel a connection to the crowd it is unreal. It's like you are on the dance floor, watching someone else DJ'*** – **Prime Cuts**

it's all gone pete tong – chronic mix fatigue

This is the trouble-shooting section! How can you save a mix that starts galloping away from you so everyone can hear? Should you save it? Yes – always! **Ali B** gives an example of how to sort it out while remaining calm and not having a blue fit or pulling a DJ strop. Remember, it's not a crime, the place won't empty because you've messed something up …

'Record A is playing; as you're bringing in record B, record A is louder because it is already playing. There's gonna be a point when record B becomes the louder of the two or becomes the most noticeable. As it's coming and it's still quiet, adjust record B, because then you won't have lost the groove. Then, when you get to the point where people are hearing record B and their attention has been diverted from record A – you need to switch the headphones and start listening to record A and adjust it.

'The worst thing you could do when you've got record B coming in is carry on adjusting it and it's getting louder and louder … you'll hear that slowing down because you're still adjusting it with your finger. So you need to get to that point when you're mixing that you swap records almost and throw your attentions on the second one. The worst thing you can do is pull the fader across. No one minds if a record goes out of time, but if you manage to pull it back in, at least you can show your skill as a DJ. It's vinyl on a deck; it's not a

computer, is it? It proves it's live, it proves that you're DJing.'

delay

When you are playing in your bedroom, you will have an ideal set-up for mixing. Your speakers will be right near the decks and the headphone volume will be audible over your stereo – you will be able to hear exactly what is going on. But when you get to the youth club or a bigger venue, it's all change, all change! In a proper club, the DJ booth will have a monitor speaker, not to be confused with the front-of-house speakers. It allows you to hear immediately what you are mixing BUT, in most cases, the monitor speakers are pretty tragic and you can't hear anything apart from the PA, drowning out anything in your headphones if you are one ear on, one ear off.

When you're playing on a big sound system, the speakers are far away from you and the sound's bouncing all over the place – it can take up to a second to get to your ear. So what's happening on the sound system is happening a second before you hear it. The mix sounds perfect to you in the headphones, but in reality, if you let it loose, a herd of buffalo would come crashing through the club. This is because you are mixing with the sound in the headphones and the PA because you can't hear the monitor speaker in the booth. However, **DJ Leon** from Flex FM slaps delay in the face with this answer: *'You've got to learn to bring it in before, so that it's too fast in the headphones, but actually it's just about right. I was playing many sets before I learned that, where nothing would go in the mix, and ended up just putting one record on after another, not mixing!'*

It will take you a few goes before you get it right and work out how much delay you are dealing with and how many beats ahead you will have to release the record. One way of getting round this is to only mix in the headphones – that way you will hear exactly what is going on and not have to worry about delay. Not everyone can, so that's why you should learn! You do need a mixer with a split cue facility though …

it shouldn't happen to a dj

So, maybe you've had a bad night, you took the needle off the wrong record, you brought all the wrong tunes with you, the promoter ran off with your money. We've all been there before …

'Any DJ that says nothing bad has ever happened to them while playing out is lying! I set the fire alarm off once from pumping too much smoke on the dance floor (the club had to be evacuated). I've had to play a set with just one hand when my top broke. And at an Ibiza Reunion the generator broke down in the middle of my set! It came

back on after ten minutes though, which was good as I was debating taking my socks off and doing a hand puppet show instead. When things go wrong, stay calm, don't panic. It's just life, don't get upset ... just laugh it off, I always do!' – **Miss Behavin'**

'I was at a nightclub in Glasgow, I got on the decks and the stylus skidded off the record. Then the monitor blew and I had to mix live for twenty-five minutes, then the needle on the other deck went, then the earphone socket blew. So, yeah, I've had a few!' – **Lisa Loud**

'Top tip! Always check your needles for dust – clubs are very dirty places. Make sure you have a record cleaner with you' – **St.John de Zilva**, DJ Workshops, who has suffered needle-skidding stunts in the past.

if you make it this far ...

Once you are a star and have a residency in a club, or maybe your small night has grown and become a regular spot on the social calendar, this is when you have to really put all the skills you have learned into practice. Now you will be playing to the same crowd week in week out, you really need to be on the ball with your choice of tunes and your use of mixing skills. You should be able to pull some cool stunts, as you will be old friends with the sound equipment by now. **Karl 'Tuff Enuff' Brown** notices some DJs still make common mistakes: *'They don't dig deep enough to find a good selection of older records to appeal to a wide range of age groups. And they don't strive to play a different set every time.'*

You have to keep the crowd interested at the same time as playing new tunes every week, or they will get bored. And you have to keep the promoter happy too or it will be back to one-off gigs for you …

last word

❛ Bob Jones said to me, "Always keep them coming back for more" ❜ – St.John de Zilva

the party's over ...

Sorry, no slow grooves here for you to chill out to – it's the end of the book. All the way through this journey you are going to make with your decks and mixer, please don't forget why you are doing it. Every single DJ in the book loves what they do. If they happen to have made it big along the way, that was an added bonus. Most of them would still do it for free. That is the secret of their success: **'Remain relevant and continue to enjoy it as much as you first did. This has to be genuine rather than** *contrived'* – **Judge Jules**

Let's hope this book has given you some inspiration to go out there and play some cool tunes and, most importantly, have a laugh with your friends. And if you hold your own night, you will know if it has been successful by the number of people still there at the end as you play that last record. They'll all be waiting for you to announce the next gig, and that's when you can be a bit pleased with yourself and think, I made those people dance, I did that, no one else. Have a warm and fuzzy moment and remember: ***'Enjoy it and go out there and relay a message because you love music!'*** – **Lisa Loud**

glossary

a

a cappella – unaccompanied singing. For DJs the term usually means a CD or twelve-inch containing purely vocal mixes.

acetate – a direct cutting of a tune on to a disc coated with a thin layer of acetate. DJs use these as testers to try out new tunes before they are pressed on to vinyl – they only last around thirty plays.

anti-skating – a feature found on professional turntables, which prevents the needle from skipping across the record.

aux. input – short for auxiliary, meaning secondary or supplementary. Plug in the Master Out lead here from your mixer.

b

backspin – spinning a record backwards while it is

playing live over the PA.

back to backing – repeating a drum break back and forth between the two turntables by using two copies of the same record, in order to extend the sample of music.

battles – competitions that turntablists enter, pitching their scratching skills against opponents, either in teams or as solo performers.

battle weapons – specially produced records with samples of drum breaks, vocals, scratching and hip-hop snippets. Used for scratching.

beat juggling – similar to back to backing, but instead of just extending the drum break, you are creating new drum patterns by manipulating the vinyl on the decks.

beat matching – the art of synchronizing and blending two separate tracks.

belt-drive deck – turntables that have their platter driven by a thick rubber band.

bpm – short for beats per minute. The bpm indicates the speed of an individual track.

c

cartridge – shortened to cart, the main component of the needle, where vibrations from the stylus are converted into an electrical impulse.

cdr – stands for compact disc recording.

channel fader – allows you to control the individual volume of each channel by the use of a slider.

counterweight – situated towards the back of the

tone arm and responsible for the amount of pressure the needle exerts on the record.

crossfader – the main component of the mixer, which allows you to fade between individual channels or play two channels simultaneously.

crossfader reverse switch – allows you to swap around the allocated channels on the crossfader; used in scratching.

curve adjust – allows you to manipulate the smoothness of the crossfader. You can either produce a perfect blend from one channel to another, or have a sharp cut-in point that is ideal for scratching.

d

dB – stands for decibel, which is the official unit used to measure the level of sound.

delay – when the sound from a club PA reaches your ears a second out of time from the record in your headphones.

desktop cd player – a single unit CD player that is usually top-loading and can be placed next to record decks.

direct-drive deck – these turntables have their platter driven directly by a motor.

dissing – short for disrespect. Used as part of battling and is usually meant in good humour – you tease/poke fun at your opponents during a battle routine.

dmc – the Dance Mix Club. Organizes the annual DMC World Scratching Championships.

drum'n'bass – started in the UK and originated from

the jungle camp. It is typically instrumental (although there may be vocals), multi-rhythmic and runs at a fast 160+ bpm. It counts reggae and jungle as its main influences. Think Goldie, Roni Size and LTJ Bukem.

e

eqs – on a mixer these dials or faders control the bass (drums), mid (vocals) and treble (cymbals) of any track. Turn them up and down to change the sound levels of the tune playing.

f

fader – see crossfader or channel fader.
flyer – a handout (usually postcard size) or a poster which advertises a club night or event.
four to the floor – a term used to describe most dance music, as it is usually made up of a four-bar beat.

g

gain (see trim) – how much an electronic circuit amplifies a signal is called its 'gain'. Sometimes mistaken for volume, the gain boosts an incoming signal (from a CD player or record deck).
garage – music that took its name from a New York club that played vocal-driven dance music in the late 70s and 80s.

h

hamster switch – another name for the crossfader Reverse Switch. So-called because it was the Bulletproof Hamster turntablist crew who invented it!

headshell – this joins directly on to the tone arm, providing a protective housing unit for the cartridge to attach to.

hi-hats – two cymbals held tightly together on a stand. The sound they produce is a much shorter sound than that produced by regular free-standing cymbals.

hip-hop – not just a style of music, but a way of life, incorporating break dancing, graffiti art, rapping and DJing/scratching.

house music – a style of dance music that originated in the 80s with a thumping bass line reinforced with a drum machine. First played at the Chicago Warehouse, Chicago, from which it took its name.

i

input selector – this is found on the mixer (normally situated alongside the channel fader) and enables you to switch from different input sources – another turntable or CD player, for example. This means that a mixer with two channels can make use of more than two inputs.

input sockets – these can be found on the back of the mixer and on other pieces of audio equipment. Other pieces of equipment can be plugged in here.

itf – the International Turntablism Federation. They hold the annual World Scratching Championships too.

j

jog wheel – the big round dial on a CD player that allows you to cue up and control pitch adjustments perfectly.

jungle – sprung out of the acid house and hip-hop music scene in the 80s. It has a thumping bass line and reggae music vocals and paved the way for drum'n'bass.

l

led – stands for light emitting diode. LEDs indicate the volume of a track by lighting up certain dB levels on the mixer.

line inputs – plug in your CD player/s here at the back of the mixer.

m

master balance – this controls which speaker the sound comes out of.

master level – normally found on the mixer, this dial controls the overall output, regardless of other volume levels.

master out – also called Line out or Booth out. This is the output from your mixer to the amp on your stereo.

mixer – one of the main pieces of equipment needed for DJing. The mixer allows you to combine two separate sound sources and play them as one.

mixing – to seamlessly blend a series of tunes together without any nasty chord or vocal clashes.

monitor – on a mixer, turn this to change the volume on your headphones.

monitor select – allows you to listen to one or both channels in your headphones.

p

pa – stands for public address system. In short, this is the equipment used to get the show on the road, such as speakers, amp, etc.

phasing – playing the same record in time on both decks and then slowing one down so that it gives a whooshing effect across the PA.

phono input – found on the mixer, this is where you plug in the phono leads from your decks. Also found on an amplifier/stereo – don't plug any phono leads in here, as you will blow up the amp.

pitch bend – allows you to speed up a track on a CD player (and some record decks) but keep the vocals at the same pitch.

pitch control/slider – a slider situated on the right-hand side of the turntable allowing you to change the speed the record is played at. Typically the pitch can be altered +/– 8%.

platter – a circular metal plate that is driven by a belt or directly by a motor.

promos – twelve-inch vinyl/CDRs containing unreleased tunes, which are sent out to DJs on mailing lists.

r

rack-mount cd player – two CD players in one unit that can be attached to a shelf above or below your record decks.

record outputs – on the mixer, these allow you to record a mix by plugging in your cassette deck/minidisk player.

rpm – stands for revolutions per minute (the amount of times the record revolves in any given minute). There are two distinct speeds – 33rpm and 45rpm.

s

scratching – the sound produced when vinyl is run back and forth under the needle. There are lots of different styles of scratching and they are combined in routines for a battle situation.

slipmats – circular pieces of felt (or plastic record sleeves!) placed between the platter and the record. The idea is that they provide just enough friction to grab the vinyl, but when the vinyl is held back the platter should still be able to rotate at the same speed.

spindle – the spike that you place the platter and vinyl upon.

stylus – also called the needle, the stylus is the minute piece of metal that reads the grooves on the record.

t

target light – a pop-up light that shines across the vinyl, allowing you to see the record in the dark.

techno – a style of music that was born in Detroit in the USA. It is a fusion of house music and funky European electronic music.

tone arm – either straight or curved, this holds the

headshell and cart. It has a counterweight attached at the back.

torque – the measurement of the power of a turntable.

trance – a spin-off from house, with a very strong four-to-the-floor bass line – lots of bleepy noises, drum rolls and peaks and troughs.

trim – another term for gain.

turntablism – the term invented by DJ Babu from the Beat Junkies, who meant it as a way of describing the use of two turntables as instruments to create music and manipulate sound.

two step – another term for UK Garage.

u

uk garage – vocal-driven spin-off from house and US garage. It drops two beats (hence two step) and has a higher bpm. Was very London-based, but is now more mainstream.

index

a

acetate cuts 22
acid house 9
Afrika Bambaataa...........7
albums 24
Ali B 16, 108
    tips from 13-14, 21,
        26, 78, 107,
        129, 131-3
anti-skate dial 37, 39
Atkins, Juan 9

b

Babu 82
baby scratch 88-9
back to backing.......... 97
backspinning 73
Bambaataa, Afrika..........7
bars 108
battling 82-3, 102-3
    battle weapon 85-6
    dissing 101-2
    preparation 99-101
beat juggling 97-8
beat matching
    ....*see mixing*
Beltram, Joey 10
Bhamra, Bob 66, 69-
    ....70, 106, 131
big beat........................12
Block, Brandon..............2,
    ....15, 18
Bobby and Steve..........14
Brown, Karl 'Tuff Enuff' ....
    ....12-13, 14, 125
    tips from 3, 57,
    ....58, 130, 136
Bukem, LTJ 12

c

cartridges 38, 39-42
cd decks 49-52
cds
    care of 27
    mixing 74-8
    versus vinyl 18-23
channel volume 43,
    ....45, 65
chirp scratch 93-4
chop scratch 89-90
clubs 107-8
courses, DJ 110-11
Cox, Carl......................10
crab scratch.............96-7
crossfader curve adjust ..
    46, 47, 84
crossfader reverse
    ....46, 84
crossfaders
    ....42-3, 45
cueing a tune
    ....57-62, 74-5

d

decks 30-2
    cartridges..........39-42
    cd.....................49-52
    parts of 36-7
    set up for scratching ..
   83-5
    tone arms 38-9, 42
    what to buy.........32-4
    where to buy.......32-6
    wiring up..............47-9
delay, speaker........133-4

dissing 101-2
Dreem Teem 13, 14,
..............................15
drum'n'bass 12, 58

e

EQs 44, 45,
...................46, 71-2
Evans, Dean 31-2
tips from..........58, 78

f

Fabio and
Grooverider 12
Fat Boy Slim................12
Femme Fatale 15
tips from.......121, 125
Fergie..................14, 116
Flare............................94
flare scratch 94-5
Flex FM 111
flyers..............108-9, 114
forward scratch 91-2
four-bar beat 55-6
Frankie Knuckles 8

g

gain control 44, 64,
...............................65
Gains, Rosie................13
garage
UK....................12-13
US....................10-11
Genius Cru................111
gigs
coping
with problems ...131-5
locations 106-10
nerves 123-5

preparation........125-7
reading the crowd
......................127-31
regular spots.....135-6
Gold, Graham 22, 55,
...................114, 115
tips from.......105, 127
Goldie 12
Grand Wizard
Theodore 81-2
Grandmixer D.ST.........82

h

hamster style
scratch 84, 89-90
hamster switch 46, 47
Hardy, Ron 8
headphones.......44, 52-4
to use or not 67-8
headshell 37, 41
Herc, Kool................7, 82
hip-hop 7-8
house music 8-9
Humphries, Tony 10-11

i

image 117-18
name and 118-19
women DJs 119-21
input selectors.............44
internet radio stations
..............................113
Invisibl Skratch Piklz
.........................85, 94

j

Jay, Norman...............111
Judge Jules 15, 16,
29, 78, 111, 117, 123

tips from..........14, 67,
.........................137-8
jungle.....................11-12

k

Kingy......................3, 116
Knuckles, Frankie 8
Kool Herc..............7, 82

l

Lamont, Matt 'Jam'......12
LED meters.....43, 45, 65
Leon.......18, 32, 62, 112
   tips from..........18, 32,
   ....33, 40, 44, 51,
   ....53, 65, 134
Levan, Larry 10, 11
Lisa Lashes.........14, 117
Lisa Loud........3, 22, 135
   tips from 5-6, 117,
   ....119-20, 121,
   ....129, 130, 138
Lisa Pin Up..................14
Livingstone, Theodore
...........................81-2
Lottie 3, 14, 117
LTJ Bukem..................12

m

Magic, Timmi..........3, 13
master balance 43-4
master volume.......43, 45
May, Derrick 9
Mikee B 13
Miss Behavin' 120,
........................124-5
   tips from..........33, 71,
   ....119, 134-5
mix tapes 113-16

mixers..............42-5, 127
   MP3......................52
   scratching.....46-7, 84
   wiring up.............47-9
mixing............57, 69-70,
  78-9
   cd.......................74-8
   changing pitch 62-4
   cueing a tune....57-62
   different tunes 64-6
   eqs.....................71-2
   headphones or not?
  67-8
   smart moves.......72-3
Mr Scruff.....................15
music
   beat structure of tunes
  55-7
   buying.................23-5
   cd versus vinyl ..18-23
   genres 6-13
   play what you love
  13-18
   promotional mailings
  25-7

n

needles 39, 40, 135

o

Oakenfold, Paul.....10, 59
Olson...........................83
   tips from..........84, 90,
   ....95, 98

p

parties....................106-7
Paulette 5, 70-1
   tips from 3, 67-8,

..... 79, 107, 120, 130
Pearce, Dave 15
phasing 63, 72
Pierre 9
Pin Up, Lisa 14
pirate radio 111-13
pitch, changing 62-4
pitch slider 37, 58
PJ the DJ 116
Plagia-wrists 40, 83,
 .... 89, 99
   tips from 38-9,
 .... 54, 88
platter 37
platter weight 37
Precise 83
   tips from 89, 91,
 .... 94, 97, 99
Prime Cuts 31, 81,
 ... 83, 99, 100, 101-2,
 .... 102, 131
   tips from ....
 .... 40, 84, 85-6,
 .... 87-8, 102-3
producing 131
promotional mailings
 25-7
Proof 83, 91

r

Rampling, Danny 10,
 .... 14, 111
rap 7-8
Run DMC 118

s

Sanchez, Roger 19,
 117-18
Sasha 3

Saunders, Jesse 8
Saunderson, Kevin ... 9-10
school gigs 107
Scratch Perverts .. 83, 102
scratching 81-3, 90-1,
 .... 98, 103
   baby scratch 88-9
   back to backing 97
   battle weapons ... 85-6
   battling 99-103
   beat juggling 97-8
   the chirp 93-4
   the chop/stab ... 89-90
   the crab 96-7
   equipment set up ....
 83-5
   the flare 94-5
   the forward 91-2
   manipulating the
    record 87-8
   marking the record
 86-7
   mixers for 46-7
   tears 92-3
   the transformer 91
   where to use 98-9
Scruff, Mr 15
slipmats 54
speakers 133-4
split button, headphone
 67
Spoony 13
stab scratch 89-90
starter kits 32-3
styli 39, 40, 135

t

tears scratch 92-3
techno 9-10
Timmi Magic 3, 13

tone arm 37, 42, 84
    setting.................38-9
torque 30, 60
trance 10
transformer scratch......91
turnablism 82-3
    see also scratching
turntables see decks

V

Van Helden, Armand
..............................13
vinyl
    battle weapons ...85-6
    care of 27
    scratching 86-7
    versus cd..........18-23
volume..................43, 44

W

Wes...........23-4, 66, 125
    tips from ...114, 128-9
women DJs .117, 119-21
workshops, DJ 110

y

Yousef...................3, 116
youth club gigs..........107

z

Zilva, St.John de
.........110-11, 112-13
    tips from ...17, 20, 70,
    ....78-9, 109-10,
    ...112, 126, 128, 135